WHO'S BUI WHERI IN KENT

Alan Major

Dedicated
to the Memory of
all those listed herein
and all others who in any
capacity great or small
have served Kent

MERESBOROUGH BOOKS
1990

Published by Meresborough Books, 17 Station Road, Rainham, Gillingham, Kent. ME8 7RS.

Meresborough Books is a specialist publisher of books about Kent with about one hundred titles available. Current list sent on request.

'A New Dictionary of Kent Dialect' by Alan Major was published by Meresborough Books in 1981. It is still available at £7.50 (£8.75 by post) in hardback.

'Bygone Kent' is a monthly magazine on all aspects of Kent history founded in 1979. It is available from newsagents and bookshops at £1.50 per issue or by postal subscription from Meresborough Books at £16.50 (£24.00 overseas) for 12 issues. Prices quoted are for 1991.

ISBN 0948193 484

Printed and bound in Great Britain by
Biddles Ltd, Guildford and King's Lynn

Introduction

It has not been, as might be thought, a morbid or miserable task to compile this book. It has proved to be one of fascinating interest, on some occasions the research being uplifting or humbling, on others humorous or near-disbelief. I am sure that few people realise, as I did not when I began, how many are the famous, infamous, notable, curious and eccentric who, by choice or through circumstances, are interred in Kent's churches and churchyards.

In Canterbury every day people unknowingly walk on the grave of a formidable woman who was captured by a French ship off the West Indies, imprisoned in a hulk, but talked her gaolers into releasing her, and who was eventually given a house to live in by the French king. Elsewhere are the graves of a vicar involved in a plot to seize Dover Castle and a rector who objected to seeing tombstones in the churchyard from his rectory windows. He started to remove them, was stopped by law, then, when he died, a large tombstone was erected on his grave in full view of the rectory windows! There is the grave of a teetotal hotel-keeper who tried to enforce his campaign of one man one drink per day and for a short time was successful, also of a doctor who eventually could no longer endure hearing of his patients' ailments and seeing them ill so he gave up practice and amassed a fortune as an inventor. A tomb contains a man who was ordered to torture an archbishop by toasting the latter's bare feet in front of a blazing fire. The first Gunpowder Plot celebration victim, a man killed by a 'rockett', is interred in Kent. There is the man who gained the Victoria Cross rescuing ship-mates from cannibals and an admiral who went 'treasure fishing' from wrecks three hundred years ago.

Another churchyard has the grave of a long-time spinster who died after fifteen days of married life, while nearby is the grave of another spinster who reached 90 through remaining unwed 'with all her faculties'. A churchyard near Maidstone has the grave of a woman who was blind but recovered her sight on Oculi Sunday, while another churchyard tomb states fully the grim details of what caused the decease of those therein.

In Kent is interred the man who recorded the hottest British temperature ever — in his back garden, another of a man who shot 8,611 varied birds, 2,079 hares and 3,764 rabbits in his lifetime until death shot him down, and an innocent man hanged at Penenden Heath.

Here are interred heroes, heroines, pioneers, inventors, artists, poets, sportsmen, politicians, a spy, a secret agent, ecclesiastics, a prince, a princess and a princess's daughter, saints, hymn writers, two kings, centenarians, smugglers, revenue men, rebels, murder and disaster victims. Also listed are tombs involved in children's customs taunting the Devil, etc. I have deliberately avoided members of the 'landed gentry', unless specially notable,

3

since they are already well-chronicled. I have concentrated in the main on lesser mortals.

The only melancholy aspect of this subject I soon realised in my research is how brief is fame or caring remembrance. The churchyard graves of people renowned in their own time are often now forgotten, neglected and over-grown. This is sometimes the case with graves of notable people in recent times. It is a sad and disgraceful reflection on modern attitudes.

Fortunately there have been instances where, even if the maintenance of the tombs or headstones is beyond the means of a parish, at least details of grave positions and inscriptions have been recorded, so these are not lost. An example is Lydd, where a booklet has been published containing all the interesting monumental inscriptions on graves in the church and churchyard, some of which have in fact since become illegible.

I hope my book will encourage more work in this direction and the recording of grave sites and inscriptions. Perhaps too it will encourage those parishes who do have graves I have listed at least occasionally to maintain each grave, by removing grass and weeds and annually cleaning the stone. Surely we owe this much to those who made rich and varied Kent's past? Where graves are being cared for I commend the church, parish council or local authority, or members of the public for their conscientiousness in doing this.

It is inevitable that some persons who should have been included in this book have been omitted for space reasons. However, if readers have details of anyone they feel ought to be added I would be pleased to receive these via Meresborough Books for inclusion in a supplement or a possible second volume.

Alan Major

Acknowledgements

To compile a book such as this would be nearly impossible without the advice and assistance of numerous other people. I have been fortunate in receiving such help and I gladly acknowledge the assistance which has been generously given to me by those listed below. Especial thanks are tendered to Kenneth Miller of Beckenham who not only researched and checked site details for the entire west and north-west Kent area, having at times to find his way through 'jungles' of grass, brambles and nettles in overgrown churchyards and cemeteries to do so, but has also provided many of the excellent photographs to illustrate this book. Equally my thanks are due to Mr L.M. Chowns of Shadoxhurst and William Smith of Ashford for supplying information concerning interments in their area and for checking details by visiting graves.

I also extend sincere thanks to all those who with courteous patience assisted me in various ways during research for this book, as follows: John E. Vigar, historian, Aylesford; Alan Dell, Edenbridge; Mrs P.J. Leibowitz, parish archivist, Lydd; R. Tate, Bearsted; Margaret King, historian, Sundridge; Michael Hardwick, Kennington; J. Clinch, Hon. Sec., Otham w. Langley P.C.C., Leeds; George Fraser, Bethersden; Irene Hales, Maidstone; Jack Bones, Eastry; A.G. Turner, Petts Wood; D. Macdonald, Dymchurch; Rosemary Hewett, Hadlow; Howard Dodsworth, Tunbridge Wells; Joan Coxhead, Borough Green; Rose Beeching, Ruckinge; Gerald Cousins, parish archivist, Cranbrook; Pauline Green, Charing & District Local History Society; William H. Lapthorne, Broadstairs; David Collyer, Deal; Enid Betts, Harrietsham; Michael Randolph, Smarden; Peter White, Benenden; Wallace Harvey, Whitstable; Tony Blake, Chestfield; M.H. Mansell, Woodchurch; Roy Humphreys, Hawkinge; W.P. Sutcliffe, Pluckley; M. Way, Hon. Records Officer, Hunton; Kenneth Meehan, Herne Bay; V. Nutting, Rainham; B. Keith-Lucas, Wye; N.E. Treliving, Farnborough Common; J.R. Hudson, Ash-by-Sandwich; P.C. A. Barnes, Community Services Dept., Kent County Constabulary, Maidstone; Rev. J. Green, Sandhurst; Rev. J.V. Russell, Selling; Rev. W. Drury, Milton Regis; Rev. P.G. Cole, Folkestone; Rev. M. Smith, Horsmonden; Rev. A. Duke, Bearsted; Rev. D. Sweetman, Eynsford; Rev. R. Goldspink, Seal; Rev. W. Hill, Lynsted; Rev. H. Walker, Dymchurch; Rev. D. Clark, Fairseat; Rev. C. Dent, Hollingbourne; Rev. A. Wagstaff, Southborough; Rev. S. Dunn, Ryarsh; Rev. J. Boyce, Brenchley; Rev. R. Ames-Lewis, Edenbridge; Rev. J. Lefroy, Upchurch; Rev. K. Prior, Sevenoaks; Rev. P. Goodsell, Sellindge; Rev. D. Marriott, Wye; Rev. R. Murch, Queenborough; Rev. M. Collis, Sutton Valence; Rev. C. Woodhead, Hoo St Werburgh; Rev. M. Bradshaw,

Boxley; the 'Bromley Advertiser'; the 'Orpington Times'; D.J. Steward, Beckenham Crematorium; Commonwealth War Graves Commission, Maidenhead; D. Cousins, Reference Library, Canterbury; L. Robards and D.R. Mole, Ref. Library, Ashford; G.B. Boreham, Ref. Library, Folkestone; S.I. Robinson, Gillingham Central Library; P. Ward, Margate Central Library; J. Maulden, Ref. Library, Tunbridge Wells; G. Fordham, Chatham Central Library; C. Crook, Gravesend Central Library; P.M. Stevens, Dartford Central Library; R.G. Purle, Rochester Library; C. Harwood, Dover Library; D.M. Laverick, Bromley Central Library; T.J. Hogarth, City Services Dept., Rochester-upon-Medway Council; H. Westgarth, Cemetery Registrar, Thanet Council; Wyn Bergess, Burnham-on-Sea; L. Pierce, Goudhurst; I.M. Woods, Milstead.

Lastly, I wish to thank Hamish Mackay-Miller of Meresborough Books for publishing this book and filling a gap in Kent reference literature.

Alan Major

ALDINGTON

Quested, Cephas (d.1821). Smuggler. A member of the Aldington Gang, he was arrested after the 'Battle of Brookland', 1821, for shooting at Revenue Officers and maiming them. Subsequently he was executed and interred in St Martin's Churchyard, Aldington, but the church authorities at that time would not allow the grave to be marked in any way. (See Ruckinge—Ransley)

APPLEDORE

Chute, Philip (d.1567). Standard Bearer to the men-of-arms of the King's Band at the Siege of Boulogne, 1544. This brought him to the notice of Henry VIII, so that he was granted the honour of bearing the lion of England on his coat of arms, given the confiscated monasteries at Faversham and in 1545 was appointed Captain of Camber Castle. Interred in the south chapel of St Peter & St Paul's Church, Appledore. In 1817 another interment, of Jeffery Munk, was made in a brick vault built in the south chapel, Chute's remains being then displaced. In 1925 during restoration of the chapel Chute's jawbone and other fragments were collected and re-interred under the window where the altar in the chapel stands. An inscription was made recording the date and year of burial, but the wrong year, 1566, was stated.

ASH-BY-SANDWICH

Goshall, Sir John de (fl.1306). His stone effigy lies on his tomb in the chancel of St Nicholas Church, Ash-by-Sandwich. Below it is the effigy of a lady, presumably his wife. Mee, in his 'Kent', makes the curious statement that the 'black woman' in a niche is 'a mysterious figure believed to have been the wife of Sir Henry Goshall who died in 1313'. The 'black woman' is not a coloured woman in that sense but was made of dark Purbeck marble.

ASHFORD

Ebsworth, Rev. Joseph Woodfall (1824-1908). Writer of ballads and lyrics, who also edited religious and historical publications. While vicar of Molash he published an exhaustive work on the annals and burial registers of the parish covering over three centuries. According to his inscription 'Devoted Twenty-Five Years of his life to the Ballad History of England' and to him we owe the complete collection of the 'Roxburgh Ballads'. Interred in Ashford Cemetery.

Fogge, Sir John (d.1490). Built the majority of the bell-tower of Ashford Church and renovated the interior at his own expense. He was Treasurer of the Household for Edward IV, outlawed by Richard III, but restored to his property by Henry VII. He also founded a College in Ashford as a memorial to the Kent people who died in the Wars of the Roses, which Edward IV endowed, but little of it now remains. Interred in a tomb on the north side of the altar of St Mary's Church, Ashford.

Smythe or Smith, Sir Thomas (d.1591). Haberdasher. 'Customer' or Collector of Custom and Subsidy on foreign merchandise for ports of Sandwich, London, Ipswich and Southampton. He was twice involved in disputes with Elizabeth I over his financial transactions, being charged with bribery, failure to keep records and peculation (embezzlement), but she was 'propitiated' by his paying her enormous rents, i.e. another form of bribery! (See Woodchurch—Waterhouse). Interred in an alabaster tomb in the south transept of St Mary's Church, Ashford. His eldest son, Sir John Smythe (1556-1608), was High Sheriff of Kent, 1600. His second son, Sir Thomas Smythe or Smith (1558-1625), merchant, was the first Governor of the East India Company, 1600.

Wainwright, William (d.1895). Superintendent, S.E. Railway Carriage and Wagon Department, Ashford. Interred in Ashford Cemetery. (See Pluckley—Board)

Waters, William (1726-1816). Known locally as 'Old William', and wife, Mary (d.1815). As recorded on their headstone they lived together as domestic servants in the same family for forty years. 'Respected and befriended by all classes of inhabitants of this town. They passed the remainder of their years contented and happy on the fruits of their honest industry.' Interred in the south-east corner, St Mary's Churchyard, Ashford, near the railings next to the footpath from Tufton Street to the High Street. (See Eastwell—Hill, Godmersham—Sackree, Kennington—Jones)

Weil, Simone (1909-1943). French mystic and philosophical author of 'Gravity & Grace'; 'Waiting on God' and 'Need for Roots', a letter written in wartime England. A doctor's daughter, as a young girl in the First World War she refused to eat sugar because soldiers at the front were deprived of it and she did not wear warm stockings because workers' children were bare-legged. During strikes in the 1930s she refused to eat more than unemployed workers could buy on relief. Accidentally burned in the Spanish Civil War when supporting the Republican Army. When Paris was occupied in 1940 she moved with her parents to Marseilles and in May 1942 they all escaped to the USA, but she soon came to England where she became a member of General de Gaulle's Free French Government. She contracted tuberculosis, which was exacerbated by her refusal to eat more than the daily rations allowed in occupied France, despite all attempts by doctors to persuade her to take food: 'I cannot eat when I think of all my people starving in France' was her reply and she continually asked for the food saved to be sent to French prisoners-of-war. She died in the former Grosvenor Sanatorium, Kennington, 24th August 1943. According to the Senior Medical Officer's Report death was due to cardiac failure due to degeneration through starvation and not pulmonary tuberculosis, but the coroner recorded a verdict of suicide while the balance of the mind was disturbed. Interred in Bybrook Cemetery, Ashford. The grave is maintained by Ashford Council.

AYLESFORD

Rycaut, Sir Paul (1628-1700). Traveller, author. He journeyed to Constantinople via Hungary, where, according to his monument, he 'remained some time in ye Turkey camp with ye Great and Famous Vizier Rupriogly'. In 1667 he was appointed Consul of the Levant Company, Smyrna and later wrote the first book on the Turkish Empire: 'History of the Empire from 1623-1677'. Interred in St Peter & St Paul's Church, Aylesford.

Thorndike, Arthur (d.1917). Minor Canon of Rochester Cathedral; Rector. Father of Sybil Thorndike, actress, and Russell Thorndike, author of the 'Dr Syn' stories. Also in the same grave are his wife Agnes (d.1933) and son Frank (d.1917). Interred in St Peter & St Paul's Churchyard, Aylesford.

BADLESMERE

Walker Children. Walker, John (d.1873) aged 65. Labourer. **Ann**, his wife (d.1874). Their Twelve Children: Eleanor (d.1838), George (d.1842), Ezekiel (d.1844), Amos (d.1845), James (d.1847), Sarah (d.1847), Mary (d.1847), John (d.1847), Thomas (d.1847), Jesse (d.1848?), Ellen Jane (d.1849), Emma (d.1850). None of their children reached adolescence. All the children are interred in one grave, the headstone being inscribed on both sides, while John and Ann Walker are interred alongside them on the north side of St Leonard's Churchyard near the church, Badlesmere. (See Cooling—Comport, Shadoxhurst—Rolfe)

BEARSTED

Fludd, Robert (1574-1637). Doctor. Author of books on the Rosicrucian Fraternity, he being a Brother of the Rosy Cross and a Master of the Rosicrucians. He wrote in Latin on philosophic science, under the name 'Robertus Flurtibus', holding some strange beliefs, such as that other creatures, vegetation, even minerals, as well as man, went to a heaven and were immortal after earthly death. Interred in the chancel of Holy Cross Church, Bearsted, a small brass plate marking the spot. A monument was originally on the south wall of the chancel (the site where the plaster was renewed can be seen) but it is now in the base of the tower.

Sondes, Freeman (1636/7-1655). Murderer. Younger son of Sir George Sondes, Earl of Faversham. On 7th August 1655, supposedly consumed by jealousy, he killed his elder brother, George, who was asleep in an upper room in the family home, Lees Court, Sheldwich, near Faversham, with a vicious blow on the head with a 'cleaver', though another source said he was stabbed. The murderer confessed immediately to his father and was taken to Maidstone next day and arraigned for trial at Maidstone Assizes on 9th August. Pleading guilty he was sentenced to death and hanged on Penenden Heath on 21st August, meeting his end with complete calm. It was supposed that they both loved the same young woman and she preferred George. Probably interred in

Holy Cross Church or Churchyard, Bearsted. According to Mee in 'Kent' Freeman Sondes 'in the churchyard lies'. Mee may have assumed that, because some of those hanged at Penenden Heath were interred in graves in Bearsted Churchyard, this was the case with Sondes. However, even though he was a murderer, the son of a nobleman would most likely have merited a simply inscribed monument of some type placed in the churchyard, but seemingly there is not. Igglesden in Vol.XIV of his 'A Saunter Through Kent' states 'the body of Freeman Sondes lies under a tomb in the church'. I have been unable to find this and Mr Robert Tate, senior lay reader at the church, has not found any trace of this Sondes and feels it certainly is not within the church. There are three possible tombs, two being late 18th century and the other an altar tomb. The one nearest to the porch is earlier, but the inscription is now illegible and it is doubtful if it is old enough to contain Sondes. However, a contemporary observer states he was interred in this church. According to an account written by Rev. R. Boreman, who, with Rev. Higgins, Rector of Hunton, attended Freeman Sondes on the scaffold, on the morning of his execution the prisoner arrived from Maidstone on horseback wearing 'mourning habit' and with many gentlemen. On arrival he calmly dismounted his horse and stood for half an hour while both divines made a discourse on his 'heinous crime'. He then said prayers and climbed the ladder, asked for the prayers of those present, said 'God's Will be done and was executed. His body after it had hung 'a good while' was cut down, put in a 'coach' and carried to Bearsted where it was interred in the church. From the evidence it was obvious Freeman Sondes was mentally deficient. His maternal grandmother was insane, and the account gives no mention of a love affair. In fact Freeman had at first pleaded jealousy, then gave various other reasons for murdering his brother. (See Throwley—Sondes)

Dyke, John, Last Man Hanged on Penenden Heath. He is reputed to be interred by or under a large Sequoia or Wellingtonia tree in Holy Cross Churchyard, Bearsted. Another source states 'the grave of the man hanged at Penenden Heath is marked by the tall Incense Cedar tree by the gate into Church Meadow'. Igglesden in Vol.XIV 'A Saunter Through Kent', 1920, states: 'In the churchyard, by the gate nearest the vicarage, is a board that covers the grave of an unfortunate fellow who was innocent of the crime of which he was found guilty over a hundred years ago. He was seen coming from the direction of some haystacks that had been set alight and on this evidence was convicted of incendiarism at Maidstone Assizes, condemned to death and hanged on Penenden Heath. He vowed he was innocent to the end . . . years afterwards the real culprit, who had emigrated to one of our colonies, confessed he was the guilty man'. Another version says the man who confessed on his deathbed was in fact a local man who had stayed in the area and because of his confession was interred in a different part of the churchyard so that his nearness would not cause offence to the innocent man. Ironically the tree-

The horizontal gravestone of Thomas Crapper in Elmers End Road Cemetery, Beckenham. (Photograph by courtesy of Kenneth Miller, Beckenham)

marked site of the grave of the innocent man is known and remembered, the site of the grave of the guilty man is unknown and forgotten. It would appear from this that the last man hanged in public on Penenden Heath and the man hanged though innocent are one and the same person. A tree was planted because, as was the case elsewhere (see Hernhill—Tom, Aldington—Quested), church authorities would not usually allow the grave of an executed criminal to be marked by a headstone and Dyke was supposedly a criminal. On checking a transcript of the 19th century burials register I found the entry: 'John Dyke hanged at Penenden Heath for arson aged 30', Dyke being interred in Bearsted Churchyard in 1830. This seems strong evidence Dyke is Igglesden's 'unfortunate fellow who was innocent'.

BECKENHAM

Bourne, Frank (d.1945). O.B.E., D.C.M. Colour-Sgt, later Lt.Col. 24th Regt, South Wales Borderers. The last survivor of the defence of Rorke's Drift, Natal, where, during the Zulu War, on 22nd/23rd January 1879, about 120 British troops successfully fought off an attack by a 4,000-strong Zulu army with minimal loss to themselves. He lived until the day after another war, that of 1939-45, ended, 9th May 1945. Interred in Elmers End Road Cemetery, Beckenham, near and facing William Evans, V.C. (See Gillingham—Bell)

11

The grave of the last V.C. winner gazetted for the First World War, William J.G. Evans, interred in Elmers End Road Cemetery, Beckenham.
(Photograph by courtesy of Kenneth Miller, Beckenham)

The large grave of Josiah Stamp, 1st Baron Stamp of Shortlands, killed during an air raid, 1941, in Elmers End Road Cemetery, Beckenham.
(Photograph by courtesy of Kenneth Miller, Beckenham)

Clerke, Jane (1726-1757). Wife of a doctor friend of the poet Thomas Gray, who composed the lines of her epitaph carved on the monument to her. This, with an urn above and carved drapery beneath, is high on the wall at the west end of the north aisle of St George's Church, Beckenham. However, this is not the original site as the church was rebuilt at the end of the last century and the site of her grave is now not known.

Crapper, Thomas (1837-1910). One of the developer-inventors and a manufacturer of the modern water-closet. Interred in Elmers End Road Cemetery, Beckenham. The metal lettering has fallen or been removed from its matrices but it is still possible to read the inscription. The six-foot long horizontal stone is clean and white among the darker, neglected gravestones.

Evans, William John George (1876-1937). C.S.Major, Manchester Regt. The last Victoria Cross winner gazetted for the First World War. He won it at Guillemont, France, on 30th July 1916, the award being published in the 'London Gazette', 30th January 1920. Interred in Elmers End Road Cemetery, Beckenham. (See Canterbury—Byrne, Gillingham—Bell, Dover—House, McWheeney, Wooden, Shorncliffe—Doogan and other V.C. winners)

Grace, Dr William Gilbert (1848-1915). General practitioner. Cricketer. Renowned as 'The Champion' for his cricket-playing prowess. First to score 2,000 runs in a season (2,739 in 1871). First to reach 100 centuries (in 1895). First to score 1,000 runs in May (also in 1895). First to reach 50,000 in a career (final total 54,896). Retired from first class cricket after 44 seasons, in 1908, aged 60. In 1895 in a match against Kent he scored 257 and 73 not out and was on the field throughout. Interred in Elmers End Road Cemetery, Beckenham. At the foot of the grave is a plaque reading 'W.G. Grace, Doctor and Cricketer, 1843-1915' also depicting a bat, ball and stumps. The cross, plinth and lettering are clean and maintained in good condition.

Stamp, Josiah Charles, 1st Baron Stamp of Shortlands (1880-1941). Economist, taxation expert, author of books on financial subjects. Chairman of the London, Midland & Scottish Railway. Director of the Bank of England. Killed with his wife Olive and eldest son Wilfrid in an air raid, 16/17th April 1941: all interred in Elmers End Road Cemetery, Beckenham.

BEKESBOURNE

Beke, Charles Tilstone (1800-1874). Explorer. He came from an ancient Kentish family that gave its name in the 12th century to Bekesbourne. Various expeditions were undertaken to Abyssinia, 1840 to 1864 and in the latter year he went to obtain the release of British subjects imprisoned by King Theodore of Abyssinia. During the following Abyssinian War his advice and maps of the area were of immense help to the British Army. He also toured Syria and Palestine, 1861-2. In 1860 he published 'The Sources of the Nile, a general survey of the basin of that river and its head streams' which assisted

The grave of W.G. Grace beautifully maintained in Elmers End Road Cemetery, Beckenham. (Photograph by courtesy of Kenneth Miller, Beckenham)

From exploring in Ethiopia to rest in a Kent churchyard. The grave of Charles Tilstone Beke at Bekesbourne. (Photograph by the author)

Speke in his quest to find the source of the Nile. Interred in St Peter's Churchyard, Bekesbourne, close to the south-west corner of the church, his grave surmounted by a red granite column.

BENENDEN

Drury, Thomas (1703-1786). Yeoman. On his headstone in St George's Churchyard, Benenden, is an hourglass and a snake swallowing its tail. (See Petham—snake on Crafts)

Mills, Richard (1798-1882). Cricketer. Played for Kent 1825-1843. Member of the Benenden Mills family that produced many fine Kent and local cricket players including George Mills who played for Kent 1825-1835 and 'brought out' E.G. Wenman. Several times the Mills family fielded an entire cricket team to play a Kent side. Richard Mills was a medium-paced round arm left-handed bowler and powerful hitting batsman. Mills and Wenman in 1834 played single-handed against an Isle of Oxney eleven at double-wicket and won by 66 runs. Wenman kept wicket while Mills bowled. In their first innings Wenman scored 65, Mills not out 84, 1 bye. Isle of Oxney first innings 55. In the second innings Wenman was not out 16, Mills 29. Isle of Oxney second innings 77. Interred in St George's Churchyard, Benenden. On the gravestone is depicted a small cricket bat and balls.

Wenman, Edward Gower (1803-1879). Cricketer. Played for Kent 1825-1854. As he stood over six feet tall he was said to be an awesome sight when batting with Fuller Pilch for Kent. The last match he played in was Veterans versus England at the Oval, 1858, when he batted with the famous Kent player Alfred Mynn. In a Married versus Single match at Tunbridge Wells, 1844, he injured a hand so batted with one hand in the second innings and scored 34, the highest score of the match! Like the Mills family his was also renowned for its cricket players, such as John Wenman (d.Benenden 1821) and John Wenman, brother of E.G. Wenman, who played for Kent in 1825 and 1837. Interred in St George's Churchyard, Benenden.

BETHERSDEN

Choute, Sir George (d.1664) and his son, also **Sir George Choute** (d.1721/2). In recording the father's burial in the parish register the then vicar, Rev. Robert Cole, wrote in verse: 'Goe sleepe Sir George. Where's such another Can equall thee? or the Squire thy brother?' Sir George had left the vicar £2 in his Will! Interred in the Frid Chapel, St Margaret's Church, Bethersden, but the fine ledger stone with the Choute Arms that marked the site was later removed from its original position and is now at the foot of the chancel steps.

In St Margaret's Churchyard at the west end is a large example of what are known as **'oven graves'**. These 'oven graves' are really a style of burial vault where arched brickwork, sometimes covered with cement or turf, covers a vault for coffins built in the earth below at normal grave level. The example at Bethersden is a three-chamber vault, up to six feet above ground level and some fifty feet in total length. There are very small gratings in the ends of two of the vaults but they do not allow viewing inside. The whole area is now heavily shaded by two large oak trees. The vaults have inscriptions on an end panel. The left-hand vault's panel (south end of the 'oven graves') states: 'This vault was built by Thomas Jackson, Esquire, of Camberwell in Surrey, in the year 1796.' The centre vault's panel reads: 'This vault was built by Edward Wilmott, Esquire, of Low Wood in this Parish in the year 1796.' The right-hand, north end vault panel has: 'This vault was built by Thomas Witherden, Esquire, of Haffenden in this Parish in the year 1796.' The Wilmotts and Witherdens were old-established families and the latter were Squires of Bethersden for several generations. It is rumoured the vaults contain funeral helmets. In Smarden Churchyard there are two separate 'oven graves' and some small 'oven graves' also occur in Biddenden and Tenterden Churchyards. (See Folkestone and Smarden)

BIDDENDEN

Nares, Rev. Edward (1762-1841). Author. In 1791 appointed Librarian at Blenheim Palace. In 1792 he was ordained and in 1798 became Rector of Biddenden which living he retained until his death. In April 1797 he had

The red marble gravestone on the grave of the Rev. Joseph Bancroft Reade, the photography pioneer, at Bishopsbourne. (Photograph by the author)

The 'oven graves' or vaults in St Margaret's Churchyard, Bethersden. (Postcard photograph c.1910 published by Everett & Ashdown, Tenterden, in the author's collection)

married, some accounts say eloped with, the third daughter of the Duke of Marlborough, the Lady Georgina Charlotte (d.1802). He remarried in 1803, his second wife being Caroline, daughter of Thomas Adams of Osborne Lodge, Cranbrook. His best known work is the 3-volume 'Memories of the Life and Administration of William Cecil, Lord Burghley', 1828-31. Other works are strangely named with odd pen-names: 'Thinks-I-To-Myself', with the pseudonym 'Thinks-I-To-Myself-Who?', 1811; 'I Says, Says I', a novel on social and fashionable life; 'Heraldic Anomalies' by 'It-Matters-Not-Who', 1823, a book of curious anecdotes. Interred in All Saints Church, Biddenden. These titles remind one of William Stevens ('Nobody') at Otham.

There are three 'oven graves' or vaults on the east side of Biddenden Churchyard.

BIRCHINGTON

Rossetti, Dante Gabriel (1828-1882). Painter. Poet. One of the artists who founded the Pre-Raphaelite Brotherhood, 1848. He married his model, Elizabeth Siddal, made famous in some of his paintings, in 1860, but she committed suicide with an overdose of laudanum, 1862. He is interred in All Saints Churchyard, Birchington, near the south porch, the monument surmounting his grave being designed by Ford Madox Brown.

BISHOPSBOURNE

Hooker, Rev. Richard (1553-1600). Author of the eight books of 'Ecclesiastical Polity'. Five of the volumes, started 1585-6, were published in his lifetime, and Book V was written at Bishopsbourne where he was vicar. The treatise is the earliest important work of this kind in English and was written to supply a philosophical and logical basis for the English Church at the Reformation settlement, a defence of the Church of England against Papal attacks. He died at the old Rectory, demolished 1954, and was interred in the church. On the south side of the chancel of St Mary's Church, Bishopsbourne, a wall monument erected in 1632 depicts him. Below it, in the floor against the wall, is a large plain flat stone, 12 feet long, supposed to cover Hooker's body. This stone was probably the original altar stone.

Reade, Rev. Joseph Bancroft (1801-1870). Photography pioneer. Microscopist. Astronomer. Chemist. Inventor. Rector of Bishopsbourne, 1863-1870. Wrote 'On Some New Organic Remains in Flint of Chalk', 1838, containing the first illustrations published in England of 'Xanthidia' (fossil dino-flagellate cysts — prehistoric marine organisms). In 1839 first used an infusion of oak 'nut galls' to make photographic paper more sensitive, an important event in the evolution of photography. He was honoured at the Paris Exhibition, 1856, for his photographs of the moon. In 1862 exhibited a 'hemispherical condenser' for the microscope that became known to microscopists as 'Reade's Kettledrum'. At Bishopsbourne invented the equilateral prism for microscopic illumination, 1869. Also at Bishopsbourne was one of the signatories of 'The Scientists' Declaration', 1864-5, a list of scientists, etc., who declared their belief that the discoveries of science and Bible teaching were reconcilable, when Darwin's 'Origin of Species' had caused upheaval among the Established Church. Interred in St Mary's Churchyard, Bishopsbourne, beneath a marble slab close to the church's north wall, alongside the path from the lychgate to the church entrance.

BORDEN

Duvard, Primogene (baptised Borden 1823-d.mid-1870s). Authoress. Eccentric. Described as 'a gaunt and eccentric spinster, who drove a donkey cart, shot rabbits and wrote religious and sentimental verses'. She lived on a plot of land at Gillingham, selling the rabbits she shot in Chatham to support herself and her mother who came from Borden. In 1842 her 'Poems' was published, followed in 1844 by 'Mary Tudor — a historical drama in 5 acts', other works being 'Devotional Exercises for Fourteen Days' and 'The Angel of Death'. Interred in St Peter & St Paul's Churchyard, Borden.

Plot, Dr Robert (1640-1696). Antiquarian. Natural Historian. He was the first Custodian of the Ashmolean Museum, Oxford, starting it with material sent back from their travels by the Tradescants. He founded the Philosophical Society of Oxford and was Secretary of the Royal Society. In 1677 his most famous work 'A Natural History of Oxfordshire' was published. He intended to cover all the counties of England and although he next started on Staffordshire the work was never completed. Interred in St Peter & St Paul's Church, Borden, beneath a rather fanciful monument that shows him as a winged warrior.

BOUGHTON MALHERBE

Sharp or Sharpe, Leonel (1559-1631). Royal Chaplain. Chaplain first to the Earl of Essex, Elizabeth I's favourite, but after Essex was executed for treason Sharpe was banished to his parish at Tiverton. He was later appointed Royal Chaplain to James I, then in 1605 to Henry, Prince of Wales. In 1614 he was confined in the Tower of London for being involved in 'controversy at Court' and fell from favour. He lived the remainder of his life at his later parish, Boughton Malherbe, where he died 1630/1. Interred in St Nicholas Church, a marble monument marking his grave.

BOUGHTON MONCHELSEA

Reiffgins, William (d.1613). Reputed to have been a beggar in the parish who eventually became wealthy and in gratitude to the parishioners of Boughton Monchelsea in his Will he left 'One annuite of four pounds by the year for 34 years to come and sixty pounds of money to be bestowed in lands to the use of the poor for ever'. Interred in an altar tomb near the lychgate of St Peter's Churchyard, Boughton Monchelsea.

Tomkin, Sarah (   ). The inscription on her gravestone states 'who having been blind for 12 years was restored to sight on Oculi Sunday, the third Sunday in Lent, 1863'. Interred in St Peter's Churchyard, overlooking the deer park, Boughton Monchelsea. (See Hothfield—Stanford; Pluckley—Hugo, Nepecker, Rucke; Stockbury—Ruffin; Sundridge—Mompesson)

BOUGHTON-UNDER-BLEAN

Francis, Elizabeth Jane (1815-1844). One of the women followers infatuated with the murderer-imposter·'Sir William Courtenay'. (See Hernhill—Tom) Daughter of George Francis, farmer, of Fairbrook House, Boughton-under-Blean, who was also involved. Interred in St Peter & St Paul's churchyard, Boughton-under-Blean. (See Kennington—Culver)

Hawkins, Thomas (d.1587 aged 101). Centenarian. The verse inscription suggests that he knew Henry VIII personally and that a convivial time was had by all. Interred in a magnificent tomb in St Peter & St Paul's Church, Boughton-under-Blean. (See Kennington—Parker; Maidstone—Fancett)

Mears, Nicholas (1805-1838). Murder victim. Killed on 31st May 1838, with pistols and sword, by 'Sir William Courtenay' at Bossenden Farm prior to the Battle of Bossenden Wood, Dunkirk, Mears being 'Courtenay's' first victim. His wife Sarah was granted a then generous pension of £40 a year for the untimely loss of her husband until her death 35 years later. Interred to the north of the nave of St Peter & St Paul's Churchyard, Boughton-under-Blean. A follower of 'Courtenay' who was killed later that day during the Battle, **George Griggs** (1819-1838), a 19 year old farm labourer, was also interred in this churchyard. (See Francis above; Hernhill—Tom; Kennington—Culver)

Spinks, Frederick Lowten (d.1899). The last Serjeant-at-Law at the English Bar, 1816. His interests were church clocks and church buildings. He donated the clock in the tower of St Peter & St Paul's Church and assisted financially in the construction of the village's other C. of E. Church, St Barnabas, built 1896 closer to the village. Interred in a tomb surrounded by railings in St Peter & St Paul's Churchyard, Boughton-under-Blean.

BOXLEY

Tennyson, Cecilia (d.1909). Sister of Alfred Lord Tennyson, Poet Laureate. In October 1842 she married Edmund Lushington, the marriage ceremony being performed by Charles Tennyson Turner, vicar of Grasby. A poet, he was the elder brother of Alfred Lord Tennyson, but had changed his name to Turner on succeeding to a great-uncle's property. Cecilia was interred with her husband in St Mary & All Saints' Church, Boxley. (See Margate—Jesse, Ker)

Lushington, Edmund Law (1811-1893). Greek Scholar. Professor of Greek at Glasgow University, 1838-75. Described in the Epilogue of Tennyson's 'In

19

Memoriam'. Brother of Henry Lushington. In October 1842 he married Cecilia, a sister of Tennyson. Interred in St Mary & All Saints' Church, Boxley. (See entry below)

Lushington, Henry (1812-1855). Barrister. Poet. Author. Chief Secretary to Malta Government 1847-55. Brother of Edmund Lushington. An early admirer of the youthful Tennyson's poetry. They met and became firm friends, 1841. In 1847 Tennyson dedicated his 'The Princess' to him. Interred in St Mary & All Saints' Church, Boxley. (See entry above and Norton—Lushington)

Sandys, George (1577-1643). Traveller. Poet. Writer. Translator. Youngest brother of Sir Edwin Sandys. (See Northbourne) In 1610 he started on a two year journey through Greece, Turkey, Syria, Palestine, Egypt, Cyprus, Crete, Malta, Sicily and Italy, returning in 1612, after which he published 'A Relation of a Journey begun 1610'. While in Egypt he visited the Pyramids and ordered his guides to fire their arquebuses ahead of them to warn off any would-be robbers! He lived at Boxley Abbey after returning from Virginia where he had gone in 1621 with his nephew, Sir Francis Wyatt, Wyatt's wife, Margaret, being Sandys' niece. While in Virginia Sandys translated Ovid. In 1638 he was appointed London agent for the Virginia Company. Interred in the chancel of St Mary & All Saints' Church, Boxley. (See Milton-by-Graves-end—Wyatt)

Wyatt, Sir Francis (1575-1644). Governor of Virginia, 1620-1626 and 1639-1643). Kinsman of George Sandys (see entry above) whose niece, Margaret (d.1644), married Wyatt. The Wyatt family had taken over Boxley Abbey after its suppression by Henry VIII. Wyatt died at Boxley and it is likely he is interred in St Mary & All Saints' Church, Boxley, although the burial site is unknown. The Dictionary of National Biography however, states: 'On 24th August 1644, Wyatt was himself buried in the family vault in the churchyard at Boxley. Margaret, his wife, who died earlier, 27th March 1644, was also buried at Boxley.' (See Milton-by-Gravesend—Wyatt)

BRABOURNE

Scott, Sir Thomas (1535-1594). High Sheriff of Kent, 1576. Commander of the Kentish armed force of 4,000 men that he raised in 24 hours to oppose the Spanish Armada. He succeeded as the heir to the Manor of Nettlestead, 1575. Interred in St Mary the Virgin's Church, Brabourne. He was grandson of the Sir John Scott (1484-1533) who had been knighted for gallantry fighting in the Low Countries, 1511. Sir Thomas Scott's second son, named after the earlier Sir John Scott was John Scott (1570-1616) who coincidentally when Captain of a Band of Lancers was also knighted for bravery in the Low Countries, 1588. He is interred in St Mary the Virgin's Church, Brabourne. He also succeeded to the Manor of Nettlestead. His first wife was Elizabeth Stafford, a descendant of a Duke of Buckingham. His second wife was Catherine Smith. In 1609 Thomas Dekker, the poet and dramatist, dedicated his 'Phoenix' to her. In Nettlestead Church by the chancel arch there are kneeling figures of Elizabeth Scott, 1598, and Catherine Scott, 1636.

A Heart Shrine. On the south side of the chancel is a small projection with a cross-incised Bethersden marble slab and a recess and reredos, built as a heart shrine, dated between 1280 and 1320 and most likely intended to contain the heart of John Balliol, founder of Balliol College, Oxford, father of John Baliol le Scot, King of Scotland and brother of Alexander Balliol, of Chilham Castle. He died in 1269 and it is known his wife had the heart embalmed in a silver and ivory casket that she wore day and night. On her death it was buried with her in the Abbey of Dulcecor near Dumfries, but the Abbey was later desecrated. John Baliol le Scot was defeated and exiled by Edward I, but had resided for a time at Brabourne and on his exile his brother probably took over ownership of the heart. It was then most likely that the Shrine was built to contain it in St Mary the Virgin's Church, Brabourne, but the Shrine is now empty.

BRASTED

Turton, John (1735-1806). Physician to the Queen's Household, 1771. Physician-in-Ordinary to Queen Charlotte, 1782. In 1797 Physician-in-Ordinary to George III and the Prince of Wales. The king gave him a clock that was formerly in a turret of the Horse Guards to put on his house, Brasted Place. Interred in St Martin's Church, Brasted, in a white marble sarcophagus.

BRENCHLEY

Ruxton, John Henry Hay (1818-1897). Captain. First Chief Constable of Kent. Ensign, then Lt., 4th Foot, 1837; retired from army service, 1843, as Captain. Appointed on 14th January 1857, as the first Chief Constable of the Kent County Constabulary, 1857-1894, at a salary of £400 a year and with a force of 222 officers and men. Died at Broad Oak, Brenchley, where there is a brass memorial tablet to him in the south transept of the parish church. Other members of the Ruxton family are similarly commemorated in the same transept of All Saints' Church, Brenchley, and at least one indicates the interment took place in the transept itself. A list of grave spaces, however, indicates that Ruxton was buried in the churchyard, but as there is an error in the numbering the position of the actual plot where he was interred is uncertain. (See Lympne—Damer Dawson; Southborough—Mitchell)

BRENZETT

Fagge, John (d.1639). The effigy of himself and one of his two sons shows one lying on his back, the other on his right side with head propped up by an arm and hand on their tomb in St Eanswyth's Church, Brenzett. Their claim to fame is that E. Nesbit, the children's author, used this curious marble tomb in one of her ghost stories. A descendant, Col. John Fagge (d.1701), fought for Parliament but later promoted the return of Charles II and was created a baronet in 1660.

BRIDGE

Kasey, Macobus (d.1512). Vicar of Patrixbourne. His half-length recumbent stone effigy — head, shoulders and hands held in prayer, is positioned in a recess low on the north side of the chancel, St Peter's Church, Bridge. At some time a portion of the wall was built across the centre of the figure thus dividing it. Kasey may have been interred beneath it originally or close by in the vicinity of the altar rails.

Montesquieu, Baron de (1750-1824). Grandson of Charles Louis de Secondat, Baron de Montesquieu (1689-1755), French philosopher and publicist. Interred in a vault near a north aisle pillar, St Peter's Church, Bridge.

BROMLEY

Johnson, Elizabeth (d.1752). Wife of Dr Samuel Johnson, known as 'Tetty'. Her epitaph in Latin was written by Johnson. An entry in the Register states: 'Elizabeth Johnson, March 26, 1752, of the Parish of St Bride, London.' The date on the stone marking her grave in fact was cut with the incorrect year, 1753. Dr Johnson was a friend of John Hawkesworth of Grete House, Bromley, and Johnson allowed his friend to make the funeral arrangements when 'Tetty' died. She was interred in the nave of Bromley Parish Church which was destroyed by bombing in April 1941, and the grave position is now unknown. During site clearance her gravestone was found and after restoration was placed in the ambulatory (turn right just inside the main entrance from Church Road) of the rebuilt St Peter & St Paul's Church, Bromley.

BROMLEY COMMON

Greig, David (1865-1952). Founder of the former chain of grocery shops. Interred, with numerous members of the Greig family, in a large grave, just inside one of the entrance gates, surmounted by a huge bronze, crouching Angel of Death, in St Luke's graveyard, Magpie Hall Lane, Bromley Common.

BROOKLAND

Plomer, John (d.1615). Three times Mayor of Romney which gave him the privilege of supporting the canopy over James I at his coronation in 1603. He was also a Burgess at Parliament and a Captain of the Select Band of Volunteers. Interred in a Jacobean altar tomb with a Bethersden marble top in the south chapel, St Augustine's Church, Brookland.

BROOMFIELD

Hatch, Joseph (1561-1639). Bellfounder. Member of the famous bellfounding family. His father Thomas was a bellfounder and on his death, 1601(?) Joseph took over the foundry that was first at Roses Farm, then later in Ulcombe parish. It is uncertain where Thomas Hatch was interred but Stahlschmidt in his 'Church Bells of Kent', 1887, states he may have returned to Broomfield on retirement to end his days. A nephew, William Hatch, took over the foundry on Joseph's retirement. William reputedly died in 1664, his place of interment being unknown, but possibly also Broomfield. In accordance with his Will Joseph was 'buryed in the parish churchyard at Bromefield beside my deare mother and brothers'. His tombstone epitaph reads 'Here lyeth the body of Joseph Hatch of Ulcombe, bellfounder, who departed this life the 14th September 1639, beside of his mother and of his brethren, aged 78 years', his brothers being Thomas and Edward. Interred in St Margaret's Churchyard, Broomfield, on the south side of the church. The table tomb was restored by a descendant of the family in 1897.

Hollands, Frederick (1822-?). Cricketer who played for Kent 1849-1859. Left-handed batsman and bowler, he delivered the ball 'slow, round-arm, twisting and rather puzzling with a high delivery (he was 6ft 2ins tall). He walked up to the crease when in the act of bowling, not advancing with a run as is the case with most cricketers'. Against the MCC & Ground at Gravesend in 1857, he took 6 wickets for 15 runs. Interred in St Margaret's Churchyard, Broomfield.

BURNTWICK ISLAND, QUEENBOROUGH

Bernard, Sidney (1818-1845). Volunteer Surgeon, R.N., H.M.S. *Eclair*. In 1845 after serving on anti-slavery duty off West Africa, where crew members contracted a very virulent form of yellow fever through which the captain, surgeon and assistant surgeon had died, the ship returned via Madeira to England. On arriving at Madeira Mr Sidney Bernard, hearing of the crew's plight and also returning to England on another ship, the *Rolla*, volunteered instead to serve on the *Eclair* and was appointed temporary surgeon. The fever-ridden *Eclair* arrived at the quarantine station, Burntwick Island in the Medway Estuary, on 2nd October 1845. Bernard was taken ill on the 3rd and died on the 9th October, by which time 74 officers and men out of a complement of 146 had died. This brave, unselfish man was interred on Burntwick Island, his grave being marked by an upright headstone reading: 'Sacred to the memory of Sidney Bernard, L/Surgeon, R.N. and son of the late William Bernard of Knocklyon House, County Dublin, who departed this life the 9th October 1845, on board H.M.S. *Eclair* whilst performing quarantine at Stangate Creek aged 27.' The headstone later fell and was broken. It was repaired and then set in concrete horizontally over the grave, with iron railings erected around it. A bronze memorial tablet set in oak was also fixed to the railings. This was re-discovered in the mud in the 1950s and housed in R.N. Hospital, Chatham, as it was then. The lonely grave is rapidly disappearing from sight in the mud of the island and now only the railings are visible at low tide. The Bernards were an old-established Irish family of Castle Bernard, Kinnitty. One of them, William Bernard (b.1792), fourth son of the 1st Earl of Bandon, was Sheriff of Cork, 1820, and M.P. for Bandon, 1832 until death 1863.

CANTERBURY

Alford, Henry (1810-1871). Dean of Canterbury, 1857-71. Poet. Hymn Writer. Two of his hymns are: 'Come, ye thankful people come' and the baptismal hymn 'In token that thou shalt not fear'. Friend of Tennyson, Arthur Hallam, Christopher Wordsworth. He wrote compositions for organ and piano and vocal music, and also founded a choral society for the cultivation of music and the singing of oratorios in cathedrals. First editor of 'The Contemporary Review'. He was responsible for restoration of the Norman south tower and porch of the cathedral and for exposing to view the Infirmary, and also for the new King's School buildings, Canterbury. The statues in the niches on the cathedral's west front were placed there after he raised subscriptions for their commission. He rescued and arranged for the two columns from Reculver (now in the crypt) to be then placed in the Baptistry garden. Interred under a yew tree on the west side of St Martin's Churchyard, Canterbury.

Anselm, Archbishop (1033-1109). Archbishop of Canterbury, 1093-1109). Interred behind the altar, St Anselm's chapel, Canterbury Cathedral.

Babington, Margaret (1878-1958). Author of 'The Romance of Canterbury Cathedral'. Editor of the 'Canterbury Cathedral Chronicle'. Hon. Steward and Treasurer of the Friends of Canterbury Cathedral, 1929-1958. The coat of arms of the Babington family is in the Cloister vaulting. She died while working at her desk on cathedral business. Her ashes were interred beneath a memorial slab on the east side of the Cloisters Cemetery. Nearby is the bay of the Cloisters restored by the Children of Kent in her memory in 1960.

Bennett, Henry Boswell (1809-1838). Murder victim. Lt. 45th Infantry Regt. Shot by 'Sir William Courtenay' during the Battle of Bossenden Wood, Dunkirk, 31st May 1838. According to a memorial tablet on the north wall of the nave of Canterbury Cathedral 'Within the Cloisters of this cathedral are deposited the remains of Henry Boswell Bennett, etc . . .' He was interred on Saturday 2nd June, with full military honours, attended by some 6,000 spectators, with three volleys being fired over the grave at the end of the funeral service, the ban on guns being fired in the Precincts having been waived by the Dean and Chapter in view of the special circumstances. (See Hernhill—Tom)

Benson, Edward White (1829-1896). Archbishop of Canterbury, 1882-1896. First Bishop of Truro, 1877. Wrote 'The 'Apocalypse', published post-humously 1900. Interred in a vault, north-west tower, Canterbury Cathedral.

Bloom, Harry (1913-1981). Campaigner for Civil Rights. Barrister. Scholar. Writer. Interred alongside Joseph Conrad (see for directions), Canterbury City Cemetery, Westgate Court Avenue, Canterbury.

Bourchier, Thomas (d.1486). Archbishop of Canterbury, 1454-1486. Great-grandson of Edward III. Archbishop through the Wars of the Roses. He crowned Edward IV, 1461, Richard III, 1483 and Henry VII, 1485. In 1486 he married Henry VII to Elizabeth of York thus uniting the two Houses of the Red Rose and White Rose. Interred in a canopy tomb in the north choir aisle near north-east transept, Canterbury Cathedral.

Boys, Sir John (1535-1612). Judge of the Claims Court of the Cinque Ports. Recorder of Canterbury. Seneschal to five Archbishops of Canterbury. Founder of Jesus Hospital, Canterbury. He is believed to have owned and lived in the tall house in Palace Street, with the leaning door and frontage, formerly the King's School shop, now commercially owned. Interred in north aisle of the nave, Canterbury Cathedral. An effigy of him reclining on the tomb is dressed in a ruff and 17th century legal robes.

Byrne, Thomas (1866-1944). Victoria Cross Winner. Private, 21st Lancers. Won his V.C. during their famous charge against the Dervishes at Omdurman, Sudan, 2nd September 1898, in which Lt. Winston Churchill took part and was an eye-witness of Byrne's gallantry, reporting it as the bravest thing he had ever seen. When a Lt. Hon. Molyneux, galloper to Lord Kitchener, was unseated and surrounded by Dervishes, although he was shot through the right shoulder and had lost his lance, Byrne, wielding his sword with his left hand, attacked and routed the enemy, prevented them from killing Molyneux and brought him to safety. Served in the South Africa War. Retired 1910. Rejoined Army First World War, serving at the Cavalry Depot, Canterbury. Interred in Canterbury cemetery, Westgate Court Avenue, Canterbury. (See Beckenham—Evans; Shorncliffe—Doogan and other V.C. winners)

Chichele, Henry (1362-1443). Archbishop of Canterbury, 1414-1443. Built the original Canterbury Cathedral library. Founded All Souls' College, Oxford, 1437. His canopy tomb near the north-east transept, Canterbury Cathedral, has 'before and after' effigies. The one on top shows him as in life wearing his canonicals, the other, below, shows him in death as a shrunken corpse. The tomb is restored every fifty years by All Souls' College, Oxford.

Coligny, Odet de (1517-1571). Bishop of Beauvais. In 1568 he had to flee to England because of his Protestant opinions. In 1571 he came to stay at the Precincts, Canterbury, in the hope of returning to France but died there after a short illness, by poison it is believed. As it was not possible at that time to

The grave of Joseph Conrad in Canterbury City Cemetery.   (Photograph by the author)

The grave of Thomas Sidney Cooper in St Martin's, Canterbury.
(Photograph by the author)

send the body to France it was placed in a temporary sepulchre of lead at the east end of the south aisle of Trinity Chapel, Canterbury Cathedral, which has stood there ever since.

Conrad, Joseph (Josef Teodor Konrad Korzeniowski) (1857-1924). Novelist who wrote novels concerned with the sea, having originally served aboard British merchant ships. His books include 'Lord Jim', 1900, 'Typhoon', 1903, and 'The Mirror of the Sea', 1906. Interred with his wife and family members in a wide grave marked by a granite column bearing Spenser's lines: 'Sleep after toil, port after stormy seas, Ease after war, death after life does greatly please.' The grave is well maintained, situated in the north-east corner, Canterbury City Cemetery, Westgate Court Avenue; path on right when entering cemetery should be followed as it curves until it turns back towards centre of cemetery, the grave being alongside the path.

Cooper, Thomas Sidney (1803-1902). Landscape and Animal Painter. He specialised in local Canterbury area scenes and very large farm animal pictures. Interred in approximately the central area of St Martin's churchyard, Canterbury.

Courtney, William (d. 1396). Archbishop of Canterbury, 1381-1396. When 39 he succeeded Archbishop Simon of Sudbury who was murdered during the Peasants' Revolt. He collected funds for rebuilding the Cathedral's belltower damaged in the earthquake of 1382. His last wish was to be interred in All Saints' church, Maidstone, but according to the information on his tomb at Canterbury he was laid to rest there in the tomb of alabaster and Purbeck marble in 1396. But the tomb for him at Maidstone has been opened and a body was seen inside. So, is the Canterbury tomb empty, or is he interred inside it and the corpse at Maidstone an imposter? The tomb at Canterbury is east of the Black Prince's tomb in the Trinity Chapel. (See Maidstone— Courtney)

Davidson, Randall (1848-1930). Archbishop of Canterbury, 1903-1928. In the north aisle of the Trinity Chapel, Canterbury Cathedral, is a cenotaph depicting him with the cope he wore at the Coronation of George V. Interred in the Cloisters Cemetery, Canterbury Cathedral.

Dunstan, St (909?(924)-d.988). Archbishop of Canterbury, 960-988, who lived through seven reigns, from Ethelstan to Ethelred, and exercised great political influence. He was made Archbishop by King Edgar but deprived of power on the accession of Ethelred, 978. He spent his last years with the affairs of the Diocese of Canterbury and the artistic and literary pursuits of his early life. He also worked to improve education and the standing of the priesthood. Interred in Canterbury Cathedral; formerly his shrine was second only to that of Becket in sanctity. Some diaper work on the south wall, above the lower flight of stairs to the altar in the Choir, may be part of St Dunstan's shrine.

Edward, Prince of Wales, The Black Prince (1330-1376). Son of Edward III. Father of Richard II. After the Battle of Poitiers, 1356, he visited Canterbury Cathedral with his prisoner, King John of France. On 10th October 1361, he married his cousin, Joan, Countess of Kent, the 'Fair Maid of Kent'. It was his wish to be interred in the crypt of Canterbury Cathedral near the chapel he had built to commemorate his marriage, now known as the Huguenot chapel, but this desire was not fulfilled. He lies in a magnificent effigy-tomb between the south piers of the Trinity chapel in the cathedral. Replicas of his funeral achievements — his jupon or coat of arms, helm and crest, gauntlets, shield and scabbard — hang above the tomb, on which is an effigy of him in armour, while the originals are preserved in a glass case at the foot of nearby steps.

Farrar, Frederick William (1831-1903). Dean of Canterbury, 1895-1903. Author. Best known for his 'Eric or Little by Little', 1858, a once-popular school tale partly autobiographical. He also wrote 'St Winifred's or The World of School', 1862, and 'The Life and Works of St Paul', 1879. Interred in the Cloisters Cemetery, Canterbury Cathedral.

Finch, Sir John (d.1660). Speaker of the House of Commons in 1629 when Members held him down in the Chair to prevent his rising and suspending the Sitting. (See Sellindge—Heyman) In 1637 he was one of the Judges who declared for the Crown in the famous Ship Money Case. Interred in St Martin's Church, Canterbury, an elaborate marble memorial inscribed in Latin being just inside the church door.

Fotherby, Dean (d.1619). Interred in a table tomb in the Lady or 'Deans' Chapel, Canterbury Cathedral, which is gruesomely horrific in appearance, due to its sides being covered with a mass of carved skulls and other human bones.

Henry of Eastry, Prior (1243-1331). Made Prior 1285, he was an efficient administrator who rebuilt the Chapter House and acted as adviser to several Archbishops. Interred in a tomb on the south side of south choir aisle, Canterbury Cathedral.

Henry IV (1367-1413). King of England 1399-1413. Son of John of Gaunt, grandson of Edward III. Known as Henry Bolingbroke, the first of the Lancastrian kings. Usurped the Crown from his cousin Richard II. His reign was notable for the number of plots and conspiracies, even his second wife being suspected of hastening his death by 'witchcraft'. Died at Westminster but was brought by barge to Canterbury, tradition stating that during the voyage down the Thames a storm arose and the panicking crew threw his corpse in the river so that the coffin was empty but covered with a cloth of gold on arrival at Canterbury. To settle the question the tomb was opened in 1832 and therein lay the king with his face still resembling the marble effigy on the tomb. Interred in a magnificent tomb with effigies between the north piers on the north side of the Trinity Chapel and opposite Edward, the Black Prince, father of Richard II, whom Henry is reputed to have had murdered. It is also said that his uneasy conscience over the death of Richard caused him to choose to be interred near the shrine of St Thomas à Becket and Richard's illustrious father, becoming the only king interred in the cathedral. Alongside him lies his second wife, Joan of Navarre (d.1437), the only queen in the cathedral. The alabaster tomb and painted canopy were erected after her death.

Holland, Lady Margaret (d.1437/9). Her superb tomb is in the centre of the St Michael's or Warriors' Chapel, Canterbury Cathedral. The daughter of Thomas Holland, Earl of Kent, she had had the tomb built to contain herself and her two husbands. The effigy on her left is that of her first husband, John Beaufort, Earl of Somerset (d.1410), son of John of Gaunt. Beaufort was the uncle of her second husband, Thomas, Duke of Clarence (d.1421), whose effigy is on her right. Thomas was Henry V's brother, and was slain in battle in Anjou fighting the Dauphin of France.

Johnson, Hewlett (1874-1966). Known as the 'Red Dean' due to his Communistic views. Dean of Canterbury 1931-1963. Interred in the Cloisters Cemetery, Canterbury Cathedral.

Kemp (Kempe), John (d.1454). Archbishop of Canterbury 1452-1454. Born at Wye, where he founded a College of Secular Canons that was dissolved at the Reformation, he acted as a diplomat for Henry VI. Interred in a tomb in the south choir aisle opposite the south-east transept, Canterbury Cathedral.

Lanfranc (1005-1089?). Archbishop of Canterbury 1070. Rebuilt the cathedral 1070-1077 after it had been destroyed by fire in 1067. Interred on the east side of the north-east transept, in St Martin's Chapel, Canterbury Cathedral.

Lang, Cosmo Gordon (1864-1945). Archbishop of Canterbury 1928, resigned 1942. In December 1936 he played an important part in public affairs, being concerned with the abdication of Edward VIII. Interred (ashes) in St Stephen's Chapel, on east side of the north-east transept, Canterbury Cathedral.

Langton, Stephen (1151-1228). Archbishop of Canterbury, 1207. In August 1213, he joined with the Barons in compelling King John to sign Magna Carta and crowned Henry III, 1216, after John was deposed. Interred in the St Michael's or Warriors' Chapel adjoining the south-west transept, Canterbury Cathedral. His stone tomb which now projects through the east wall of the chapel was originally within the apse of the old Norman chapel of St Michael. The wall was arched over it so that the Archbishop's remains would rest beneath the altar when the chapel was reconstructed to contain the tomb of Margaret Holland.

Manwood, Sir Roger (1525-1592). Judge. M.P. for Sandwich 1557-1572. Judge of the Chancery and Admiralty Courts of Dover. With Archbishop Parker he founded a Grammar School at Sandwich, which replaced another school that had been suppressed in 1547. In later years he fell out of favour with Elizabeth I (who had granted him the royal manor of St Stephen's, Hackington) for offences that we would call 'bending the law' and for offering bribes to obtain various offices. He built almshouses at St Stephen's and a new transept, the south, in St Stephen's Church wherein he is interred. The tomb has a bust of Sir Roger showing him wearing the SS collar, as the first Chief Baron of the Exchequer to receive this honoured decoration. The collar, shaped like a letter S, is still worn by the Lord Chief Justice. The macabre feature of the tomb is a full-size replica of a skeleton lying on its back at the base and as the tomb was erected in his lifetime he must have looked on this scene where he would eventually lie.

Maugham, Somerset William (1874-1965). Novelist. Short Story Writer. Playwright. He was a boarder at King's School, Canterbury, and some of his early life was spent at Whitstable. His ashes are interred in the King's School grounds, near the Library which he donated.

Meopham, Simon. Archbishop of Canterbury, 1327-1333. Benefactor to the poor; by his order Wills of serfs' possessions worth less than 100 shillings were registered without a fee. His tomb may have in its unusual form some of the memories of Becket's 'tumba' when in the crypt. The black marble tomb forms a screen to St Anselm's Chapel at the east end of the south choir aisle, Canterbury Cathedral.

More, Sir Thomas (1478-1535). Lord Chancellor in the reign of Henry VIII, he refused to take the oath of Supremacy and was executed by beheading on Tower Hill, his head being rescued by his daughter Margaret Roper. He was author of 'Utopia', 1516, a philosophical romance describing an ideal society. Every 6th July, on the anniversary of his death, a United Service for Christ and Christian Unity is held in St Dunstan's Church, Canterbury, where his head only is interred in the Roper family vault beneath the St Nicholas (alias Roper) Chapel where a commemorative marble slab was placed in 1932.

Morton, John. Archbishop of Canterbury 1486-1500. He is praised by Sir Thomas More in the latter's 'Utopia'. The tomb in the crypt is an empty cenotaph as, according to his last wish, he was buried under a large marble slab in the nearby Chapel of Our Lady Undercroft, Canterbury Cathedral.

Newham, James William (1825-1890). Clerk, Maidstone Prison, 1851. Deputy Governor, Maidstone Prison, 1858. Governor, Canterbury Prison, 1878. Interred in St Martin's Churchyard, Canterbury, on east side under a yew tree, the headstone being in a very poor condition.

Packe, Dr Christopher (1686-1749). Physician. Author. He wrote the curious 'A Dissertation Upon the Surface of the Earth as Delineated in a specimen of a Philosophico-Chorographical Chart of East Kent', 1737, that had been presented to the Royal Society in 1736 for their approval. He improved this as his 'Convallium-Descriptio, an explanation of a new Philosophico-Chorographical Chart of East Kent', 1743, the chart containing 'A graphical delineation of the country 15 or 16 miles around Canterbury'. For this he had climbed the Bell Harry Tower of the Cathedral to take bearings. He practised in Canterbury 25 years and was involved in a contentious publicised controversy with a Dr John Gray of Canterbury regarding the treatment of Robert Worger of Hinxhill who fell from his horse and later died of 'brain concussion'. Worger's relatives were not satisfied with Packe's treatment of him and called in Gray and two surgeons, who, Packe alleged in letters in the 'Canterbury News-Letter' of 8th and 15th October 1726, killed the patient with excessive bleeding and trepanning. Interred in St Mary Magdalene's Church, Canterbury. His son, also Christopher and a physician (d.1800) practised in Canterbury and is interred alongside his father.

Parry, Edward (1830-1890). Son of Rear-Admiral Sir William Parry, Arctic explorer. Appointed Suffragan Bishop of Dover, 1870, to assist the Archbishop of Canterbury. This had been a Tudor office — the previous holder of it died in 1597, but it was revived in the 19th century to take some of the administrative work from the Archbishop. His cenotaph is in the north aisle of the nave, Canterbury Cathedral. Interred on the east side, close to Church (near Newham), St Martin's Churchyard, Canterbury.

Peckham (Pecham), John. Archbishop of Canterbury 1279-1292. Doctor, obtaining his degree at Paris University. He wrote numerous books on theology and science, including a treatise on optics which was reprinted several times. Interred in a tomb under the Edward IV window, north-west transept or Martyrdom, Canterbury Cathedral. On his tomb is a wooden effigy, originally decorated with gesso, gilding and colour, the oldest effigy in the cathedral.

Pilch, Fuller (1803?4?-1870). Cricketer. Played for Kent (last game 1854), then was groundsman at Canterbury until 1868. In the year of his death the sporting public subscribed for the obelisk, erected 1871, originally marking his grave in St Gregory's Churchyard, Canterbury. In 1922 K.C.C. placed a bronze plaque on the memorial, showing Pilch at the wicket, taken from G.F. Watts' famous lithograph of him. The grave obelisk is now sited in the K.C.C. ground, Canterbury, to preserve it.

Pole, Reginald (1500-1558). Cardinal. Statesman. The last Roman Catholic Archbishop of Canterbury. Opposed Henry VIII over his divorcing Catherine of Aragon and fled to the Continent for safety, 1531. He returned to England on the accession of Catholic Mary I, 1553, as Papal Legate, and then became

Archbishop, 1556, on the death at the stake of Cranmer. Interred in a simple tomb on north side of the Corona, Canterbury Cathedral.

Rooke, Sir George (1650-1708/9). Admiral. In 1702 he was Commander of the expedition that captured or destroyed the Spanish treasure ships and French warships in Vigo Bay. In 1704, with Sir Cloudesley Shovell, he captured Gibraltar. Interred in St Paul's Church, Canterbury.

Roper, William (1496-1578). Biographer of Sir Thomas More (see above), his work being the chief source of information concerning More's personal history. M.P. for Canterbury 1555, 1557-8. Fell from favour on death of Mary I. He married More's eldest daughter, Margaret, 1525. It was possibly she who purchased her father's head after execution, and some sources claim it was interred with her in Chelsea Church. Or is the head in a lead box found in the Roper Vault where William Roper was also interred in St Dunstan's Church, Canterbury? (See Farningham—Roper; Lynsted—Roper)

Sheppard, Very Rev. Hugh Richard Lawrie (1880-1937). Famous as 'Dick' Sheppard when Vicar of St Martin's-in-the-Fields, London, 1914-1927, where he had a reputation for his broadcast sermons that attracted large congregations and numbers of radio listeners. Dean of Canterbury 1929-1931. Interred in the Cloisters Cemetery, Canterbury Cathedral.

Shipley, Dame Mary (1732-1820). Wife of Sir Charles Shipley (1755-1815), General, Royal Engineers; Governor of Grenada, West Indies, 1813, whom she married at Gravesend, 1780. On one of his various military appointments in the West Indies while off Barbados he and his wife Mary were captured by a French corvette and imprisoned in a hulk at Guadeloupe. The formidable Mary, however, was soon released and eventually, after hearing her personal petition, the French General in command also released her husband, who died and was interred in Grenada, 1815. In recognition of her husband's services in the French West Indies Louis XVIII assigned her a residence in Boulogne and when she died in 1820 she was interred in the English Cemetery there. In 1831 she was exhumed and being the grand-daughter of Canon Ralph Blomer (d.1732, interred in the cathedral), Chaplain to Charles II and Prebendary of Canterbury Cathedral, she was re-interred on the paved north side of the Cloisters, Canterbury Cathedral. The slab covering her grave is now becoming badly worn by the feet of pedestrians who daily walk on it.

Somner, William (1598-1669). Antiquary. Anglo-Saxon Scholar. His earliest work is 'The Antiquities of Canterbury or a Survey of that Ancient Citie with the Suburbs and Cathedral', 1640. Started on a History of Kent but abandoned it on the outbreak of the Civil War. In 1647 completed 'A Treatise of Gavelkind, both Name and Thing'. He also made an English translation of 'The Ancient Saxon Laws' published in Latin by William Lambarde. Interred in St Margaret's Church, Canterbury.

Mary Tourtel's grave in St Martin's Churchyard, Canterbury.
(Photograph by the author)

Stratford, John (d.1348). Archbishop of Canterbury 1333-1348. In 1327 he took part in deposing Edward II and drew up a document telling why he had been deposed. Chief adviser to Edward III but fell from favour in 1340, being blamed for the failure of an expedition to Flanders. He defended himself against this blame and established the precept that peers should only be tried before their own order in full Parliament. Interred in the south choir aisle, Canterbury Cathedral.

Sudbury, Simon. Archbishop of Canterbury 1375-1381. Beheaded on Tower Hill during Wat Tyler's rebellion. His tomb at the east end of the south choir aisle in Canterbury Cathedral contains only his torso with a ball of lead in place of his head. The latter is preserved in Sudbury Church, Suffolk.

Temple, Frederick (1821-1902). Archbishop of Canterbury 1897-1902. Leading figure in the Temperance Movement. Father of William Temple, also Archbishop of Canterbury. Interred in the Cloisters Cemetery, Canterbury Cathedral.

Temple, William (1881-1944). Archbishop of Canterbury 1942-1944. By his public speeches and radio broadcasts he did much to sustain the morale of the British people during the Second World War years, his incumbency being overshadowed by his own ill-health. Wrote 'Nature, Man & God', 1932-34. Interred in the Cloisters Cemetery, Canterbury Cathedral.

Tourtel, Mary (née Caldwell) (1874-1948). Artist. Creator of Rupert Bear, the famous newspaper and Annual book character commissioned by her husband, Herbert Bird Tourtel (1874-1931) in 1920 when he was deputy editor of the Daily Express. Both interred on the east side of St Martin's Churchyard, Canterbury.

Wace, Henry (d.1924). Dean of Canterbury 1903-1924. Wrote numerous religious and learned books, also edited the 'Dictionary of Christian Biography during the First Eight Centuries', 4 vols., 1877-1887, and 'Dictionary of Christian Biography during First Six Centuries', 1 vol., 1911. Interred in the Cloisters Cemetery, Canterbury Cathedral.

Walter, Hubert. Archbishop of Canterbury 1193-1205. Accompanied Richard I to the Holy Land on the Third Crusade. He negotiated with Saladin the truce of 3 years, 3 months, 3 weeks, 3 days. Raised the ransom of £100,000 to secure the release of Richard imprisoned by the Emperor of Germany. Interred in the aisle to the south of the Trinity Chapel, Canterbury Cathedral, his being the oldest tomb in the cathedral.

Warham, William. Archbishop of Canterbury 1503-1532. Friend of Erasmus, the Dutch scholar, who dedicated to him and to Leo X his edition of the New Testament in Greek, the first ever published in print. Interred in a tomb under the Edward IV window of the north-west transept or Martyrdom, Canterbury Cathedral.

Wotton, Nicholas (d.1567). First Dean of Canterbury after the Dissolution had banished the Prior and monks. Simultaneously Dean of York he held both positions during the reigns of Henry VIII, Edward VI, Mary I and Elizabeth I. He was also a Privy Councillor, Secretary of State, Ambassador to France, Spain and Flanders, and was one of those sent to arrange the marriage between Henry and Anne of Cleves, 1539. Fortunately for him he had advised the king in letters that Anne's feminine beauty and personal accomplishments were not up to the high standard the king demanded. Interred in a fine Renaissance tomb that bears his kneeling figure, in the north aisle of the Trinity Chapel, Canterbury Cathedral.

CHARING

Dering, Christopher (1625-1693). Secretary to Heneage Finch, Chancellor of England and Earl of Nottingham. Interred in St Peter & St Paul's Church, Charing, in the Brent family chapel, from whom the Wickins estate, Charing, had come to the Derings by marriage.

Honywood, Sir Robert (1601-1686). Politician. Translator. Served on the Continent in the Wars of the Palatinate with rank of Colonel. Sent on a political mission to Sweden, but recalled at the Restoration, 1660. In 1673 translated and published 'The History of the Affairs of Europe, but more Particularly of the Republick of Venice', by Battista Nani. Apparently Honywood began translation work in his old age, being in dire straits after his son had failed to obey the Proclamation of 1666 recalling Englishmen serving in the army of Holland so that the Honywood property at Charing had been confiscated. Interred at Charing according to the 'Dictionary of National Biography'. There is a monument commemorating him and his wife.

Loftus, Thomas (1752-1804). Soldier. Quartermaster, 43rd Regt. of Foot. He fought and was wounded at the Battle of Bunker Hill, 1775, between the British Army and the Americans. Served in the same Regiment for 14 years, 51 weeks, 6 days, in England, Scotland, Ireland, Guernsey, America (9 years, 37 weeks, 6 days) and West Indies, as his gravestone records. Interred near the entrance to St Peter and St Paul's Church, Charing.

Stuart, Ronald Neil (1886-1954). Victoria Cross Winner, also D.S.O. 1st Lt., (later Capt.), R.N.R. He was awarded his V.C. for bravery in the action between 'Q ship' H.M.S. *Pargust* and the UC 29 on 7th June 1917. Captain of the CPR *Empress of Britain* and Commodore of the CPR Fleet 1934. Interred in Charing Cemetery.

CHARTHAM

Reading, John (d.1667). Chaplain to Charles I. In 1643 appointed Rector of Chartham by Archbishop Laud, but was not instituted and having been also deprived of the living at St Mary's Church, Dover, was involved in a plot to seize Dover Castle, being imprisoned in Leeds Castle for his part in the conspiracy. There he wrote a thesis 'A Guide to the Holy Citie', that helped gain his release and reappointment to his Dover benefice. He even spoke the Address of Welcome when Charles II landed at Dover on his Restoration, 1660. That same year he was also re-appointed Rector of Chartham and made Rector of Cheriton. Interred in St Mary's Church, Chartham.

CHART SUTTON

Unknown Battle of Britain Pilot's Grave. At Parkhouse Farm a Hurricane crashed on 3rd September 1940, the fragmentary remains of the pilot being removed for burial. An elderly couple living in a farm cottage nearby created there what is now the Pilot's Memorial Garden maintained by Headcorn Branch, R.A.F.A. since 1970, with an annual service and flypast held on the Sunday preceding Battle of Britain Sunday in September. At Chart Sutton near Maidstone.

CHATHAM

Kellaway, Joseph (1824-1880). Victoria Cross Winner. Boatswain, 3rd Class, H.M.S. *Wrangler*. He was awarded the V.C. when it was instituted on 29th January 1856, at the close of the Crimean War, following an incident at

French Prisoners of War Cemetery, former Royal Naval Barracks, Chatham, c.1908.
(Photograph in author's collection)

St George's Church, former Royal Naval Barracks, Chatham, c.1908. On the left can be seen the French prisoners of war cemetery with its monument in their memory.
(Postcard in the author's collection)

Mariupol, Crimea, on 31st August 1855. He received his award personally from Queen Victoria, as did 61 other V.C. winners, at the first investiture of the medal in Hyde Park on 26th June 1857. Also receiving his V.C. that day was Mate, later Lt., Charles Lucas (see Mereworth—Lucas). Interred in Chatham Cemetery, Grave 579, Section N, parallel with Maidstone Road, Chatham.

McCudden, William (1891-1915). Sergeant, Royal Flying Corps. Brother of James McCudden, V.C. and John McCudden, also First World War pilots, both interred in France. William McCudden was flying a Bleriot trainer on 1st May 1915 at Gosport, when it stalled and crashed and he was killed. On May 5th 1915 he was interred in Chatham Cemetery in the McCudden family grave, Section CC, marked by a large black full-kerbed memorial surmounted by a cross.

Alongside St George's Church (former H.M.S. *Pembroke,* R.N. Barracks, Chatham) is a cemetery for Napoleonic French prisoners of war, with a monument in their memory. About 500 bodies were interred there after removal from St Mary's Island at the turn of the century and some of the remains were also recovered from the site of Gillingham Gas Works. The cemetery, since the closure of the Barracks, has become neglected and overgrown with trees and shrubs.

CHELSFIELD

Crosby, Brass (1725-1793). Lord Mayor of London 1771. On receiving office one of his first acts was to refuse to support the issuing of warrants for Press Gangs and he ordered constables to be positioned 'at all avenues' of the city to prevent Press Gangs seizing men. He had a famous battle with the House of Commons over publishing Parliamentary Debates. In 1771, when Chief Magistrate, he had brought before him a printer who had dared to publish reports of Parliamentary proceedings. He released the man whereon Crosby was ordered to appear in the House of Commons to explain his action. He was committed to the Tower of London, but when brought to trial several judges refused to hear the case and after protests from the public Crosby was released. After this no further attempt has ever been made to prevent publication of the Debates. The saying 'as bold as brass' is said to have originated from this encounter. He married Mary, daughter of James Maud of Chelsfield, also interred in St Martin of Tours Church, Chelsfield, near Orpington.

Maud, James (d.1769). Father of Mary Crosby (see above entry). On the south side of the nave of St Martin of Tours Church, Chelsfield, is a stone plaque memorial 'to the memory of James Maud, Esq., Lord of the Manor of Chelsfield, who died July 19th 1769. This monument was erected by his only daughter, Mary Crosby, Relict (widow) of the late Alderman Crosby. She died 6th October 1800. And in a vault underneath her remains with theirs are united'. This indicates Brass Crosby, his wife Mary and father-in-law James Maud are all interred in Chelsfield Church.

CHERITON

Chisman, Francis (d.1664). Affixed to the north wall of the Enbrook Chapel is the Chisman monumental stone, of which the last two lines of the inscription refer to chimney tax or hearth money. His death came two years after it was introduced in 1662. It was a tax laid on hearths in all houses paying the church and poor rates, but it was repealed in the reign of William & Mary. The stone is almost indecipherable now. In St Martin's Church, Cheriton. (See Folkestone—Rogers)

CHEVENING

Stanhope, Charles, 3rd Earl Stanhope (1753-1816). Politician. Scientist. Inventor. He experimented with safeguarding buildings from fire by using a 'stucco' on the exterior. In 1790 he obtained patents for two steam driven vessels. A curious project in 1795 was for propelling boats on water with 'ducks-feet oars', but the highest speed obtained was 3 m.p.h. He perfected a system of stereotyping for the printing craft, acquired by the Clarendon Press, Oxford, in 1805. He also invented an iron hand-printing-press, the Stanhope Press, which they also acquired. Many printing firms later had the press, even into the 20th century, principally used then for proofing. Other inventions included a lightning conductor, two calculating machines, a microscopic lens, a new type of cement claimed to be more durable than ordinary mortar, and an artificial tile for house roofing. He married William Pitt's sister, Hester, in 1774. Interred in the family vault in St Botolph's Church, Chevening.

Stanhope, James, 1st Earl Stanhope (1673-1721). Soldier. He spent his early years in Spain with his father and the knowledge of the country he acquired then was put to good use at the siege and capture of Barcelona, 1705. He also took part in other Spanish campaigns. Interred with full military honours in St Botolph's Church, Chevening.

CHIDDINGSTONE

Streatfeild, Thomas (1777-1848). Topographer. Genealogist. Artist. He formed a collection of material, manuscripts and specimens for a History of Kent and spent £3,000 on commissioning drawings from various artists as illustrations, but it was not published by him. A prospectus he sent out received little interest from the public. On his death the manuscripts and illustrations, together with his own drawings (he was a skilled artist) went by bequest to Lambert Larking (for which see—Ryarsh) for his disposal. Streatfeild's collection, totalling 52 volumes, is now in the British Museum. Interred in St Mary's Churchyard, Chiddingstone.

CHILHAM

Hardy, Arthur and **Edmund** (d.Chilham Castle, October 1858). Sons of Charles Hardy, then owner of the castle and estate. On the north side of the chancel of Chilham Church is a fine portrait sculpture, unique in England, showing the two boys reading from a book engraved with a scene from 'Babes in the Wood' with their battledore and shuttlecock lying at their feet. It was originally commissioned by their father to stand in the castle but when the Hardy family left Chilham in 1919 it was given to the church. The Hardy graves are in a railed-off area on the east side of St Mary's Churchyard, Chilham, where there is a gravestone to **Charles Hardy** (1813-1867) so it is possible the two boys are also interred therein.

CHISLEHURST

Campbell, Sir Malcolm (1885-1948). Racing driver. Land and Water Speed Pioneer. He held the land speed record of 310 m.p.h., 1935, and water speed record 141.7 m.p.h., 1939. Interred in St Nicholas Churchyard, Chislehurst.

Sydney, John Robert, 3rd Viscount, 1st and Last Earl Sydney (1805-1890). Lord Chamberlain. Later Lord Steward of Queen Victoria's Household. Interred in the Scadbury Chapel, St Nicholas Church, Chislehurst. The figure of Earl Sydney was begun by Sir Edgar Boehm and completed by Alfred Gilbert.

Walsingham, Sir Edmund (1490-1549/50). He attended Henry VIII at the Field of the Cloth of Gold, 1520. In 1525 he was appointed Lieutenant to the Tower of London by Henry and held the office 22 years, having personal charge of prisoners of state including Anne Boleyn and Sir Thomas More. His son, Sir Thomas Walsingham (1526-1584), Sheriff of Kent, 1563, erected the monument to him, 1581, in the Scadbury Chapel, St Nicholas Church, Chislehurst, where Sir Edmund is interred. Interred in the same chapel is Sir Edmund's father, **James Walsingham** (d.1540) who was Sheriff of Kent, 1497.

Walsingham, Sir Thomas (1568-1630). Third son of Sir Thomas Walsingham (1526-1584). A favourite of Elizabeth I who visited him at his mansion, Scadbury, Chislehurst, 1597. Keeper of the Great Park of Eltham, 1599. On the death of Elizabeth he and his wife were appointed Keepers of the Queen's Wardrobe to James I's wife Anne and he was M.P. for Rochester 1597 to 1626. A patron of the arts and literature, in 1593 he gave asylum to Christopher Marlowe at Chislehurst. Marlowe dedicated his poem 'Hero and Leander' to him and in return Walsingham bestowed many favours on Marlowe and other poets. Interred in the Scadbury Chapel, St Nicholas Church, Chislehurst.

Warwick, Sir Philip (1609-1683). Soldier. Lawyer. Politician. Historian. He served in Charles I's army as a Volunteer at the Battle of Edgehill. As

Sir Malcolm Campbell's grave, Chislehurst.   (Photograph by
courtesy of Kenneth Miller, Beckenham)

William Willett's grave, also at Chislehurst.   (Photograph by
courtesy of Kenneth Miller, Beckenham)

Secretary to Charles I he was entrusted with details of State matters that
Warwick later published with details of the trial and execution of Charles I.
He lay low during Cromwell's regime which fined him heavily for supporting
Charles. In 1661 he was made Secretary to the Lord High Treasurer because
he was 'an incorrupt man who during 7 years in the management of the
Treasury made but an ordinary fortune out of it.' Interred in St Nicholas
Church, Chislehurst.

Willett, William (1856-1915). A builder by trade who tirelessly advocated the
Daylight Saving Scheme which would give an extra hour of daylight in
summer. He died just before British Summer Time was put into effect, as a
wartime measure, in 1916. Interred in St Nicholas Churchyard, Chislehurst.
There is a memorial sundial to him in Petts Wood.

Wollaston, William Hyde (1766-1828). Mineralogist. Chemist. Physiolo-
gist. Physicist. Astronomer. Botanist. He began as a general practitioner but
due to an over-sensitive nature concerning his patients and their ailments he
gave up practice to do chemical and other research. He discovered a process
for making platinum malleable that he kept secret until his death and from this
and other royalties for processes he devised he gained a fortune of £30,000. He

40

discovered palladium in the platinum ores and also a method of producing pure platinum and welding it into vessels that was of great importance for the concentration of sulphuric acid for vitriol makers. In 1803 he invented 'periscopic' spectacles, useful when oblique vision is necessary and in 1807 patented the camera lucida valuable in surveying and copying drawings and drawing objects under the microscope. Interred in St Nicholas Churchyard, Chislehurst.

COBHAM

Brooke, William (buried 1597). 7th Lord Cobham, descended from the ancient Lords of Cobham through the female line. A favourite of Elizabeth I, he twice entertained her at Cobham Hall on her 'progress' through Kent in 1559 and 1573. His offices included Lord Warden of the Cinque Ports, Lord Lieutenant of Kent and Constable of the Tower of London. Interred in St Mary Magdalene's Church, Cobham. His son was Henry Brooke, 8th Lord Cobham, the conspirator (d.1619) involved with Sir Walter Raleigh in communicating with the Spanish Ambassador Aremberg to place Arabella Stuart on the English throne and kill the 'king and his cubs'.

COOLING

The Comport Children. A line of small gravestones of the 18th century Comport children in St James the Greater's Churchyard, Cooling, gave Dickens the idea for the tombstones of Pip's dead brothers in 'Great Expectations', 1860-61. 'Pip' refers to five little stone lozenges sacred to the memory of five little 'brothers of mine', but there are thirteen lozenge-shaped stones commemorating various Comport children, none of whom was older than 17 months at death. Malaria was possibly the cause. (See Badlesmere—Walker children; Shadoxhurst—Rolfe children)

CRANBROOK

Beeman, Rev. Isaac (1765-1838). Minister of the Gospel for many years at the Providence Chapel, Cranbrook, which is still in existence, having been bought in London in the early 19th century and transported by road for erection on its present site. It was extended in 1828 with the addition of a circular frontage to house the increasing congregation. Their voluntary subscriptions paid for the tomb of Isaac Beeman in St Dunstan's Churchyard, Cranbrook, some six feet away from that of Alexander Courthope.

Courthope, Alexander (d.1608). Clothier. One of the oldest still legible tombstones in a Kent churchyard (see Hollingbourne—Reynolds; Stockbury—Gover) reading: 'Here lieth the body of Alexander Courthope of Goddards Green in this parish who was buried September 13th 1608. Also the body of Elizabeth his wife who was buried January 19th before. They had issue 11 sons and 5 daughters. In the year 1765 this tomb being much decayed by time was repaired by Alexander Courthope, of Sprivers, Horsmonden, a descendant in the fourth generation from Alexander and Elizabeth Courthope here interred.' These details of the inscription are on a marble slab on the south side of the table tomb in St Dunstan's Churchyard, Cranbrook.

Dennett, John Thomas (1806-1890). Cranbrook Publisher and Bookseller. He published 'The Annals of Cranbrook Church', by William Tarbutt, 1870 (see following entry). Local Agent for the Kent Fire Office who was involved in his capacity as Agent in the Great Fire at Cranbrook, May 1840, when the premises of an upholsterer cabinet and chair maker caught alight. Interred in St Dunstan's Churchyard, Cranbrook. Near him, with one other Dennett tombstone separating them, lies his sister, who died 101 years previous to him! She was born in 1775 and died aged 14 years 11 months, on 6th March 1789. This circumstance was due to the sister being a child of a first marriage and her brother being the youngest son of a second marriage.

Tarbutt, William (1810-1893). Cranbrook Historian. He gave lectures which were published by J.T. Dennett in 1870 as 'The Annals of Cranbrook Church'. Interred in St Dunstan's Churchyard, Cranbrook.

Thatcher, George (1676-1754). Clockmaker. Interred with his wife Constant (d.1743/4) in St Dunstan's Churchyard, Cranbrook.

Webster, Thomas, R.A. (1800-1886). Artist. Painted scenes of school, schoolboys and village life. Examples: 'Released from School', 'The Truant', 'The Village Choir', 'The Boy With Many Friends', as well as paintings including local scenes. The last 30 years of his life were spent at Cranbrook where he died. The founder-member of the colony of Cranbrook artists that included J.C. Horsley, A.E. Mulready, Frederick D. Hardy, George Hardy and G.B. O'Neill. He left £2,000 in his Will to the Queen Elizabeth's Grammar School, the annual income of which was to found two scholarships for pupils at Cambridge University, tenable for three years, though unfortunately there have not always been Old Cranbrookians at Cambridge. Over a period of time permission was gained from the Ministry of Education for these funds to go to students at universities other than Cambridge, then in 1948 to entrance scholarships to Cranbrook School. Interred in St Dunstan's Churchyard, Cranbrook, the inscription being partly legible. (See Dymchurch—Bedingfield)

CRANBROOK — GLASSENBURY PARK

Jaffa. Napoleon's favourite charger, ridden by him at the Battle of Marengo, 1800, named after the Battle of Jaffa Port, 1799. Interred at Glassenbury Park where the horse's grave is marked by a stone column. Died 1826, aged 37. How he came to Glassenbury is uncertain, but General Beresford, in charge of Wellington's quartermaster arrangements, retired to Bedgebury Park and possibly Jaffa had come under his jurisdiction after Waterloo and eventually the horse ended its days at Glassenbury.

The headstone of Peter Isnell (the Amen man) at Crayford. (Photograph by courtesy of Kenneth Miller, Beckenham)

CRAYFORD

Isnell, Peter (d.1811). Parish Clerk. Interred in St Paulinus Churchyard, Crayford, the grave being 60 feet south of the church tower. His epitaph in the church porch has verses worth recording herein:

'Here lies the body of Peter Isnell. Thirty Years Clerk of this Parish. He lived respected. A Pious and Worthy Man and died on his way to officiate at a wedding, on 31st August 1811, aged 70 years. The inhabitants of Crayford raised this stone to his Cheerful Memory and as a tribute to his faithful service.

'The life of this Clerk was just threescore and ten
Nearly half of which time he had sung Amen;
In his Youth he was Married like other young men
But his wife died one day, so he chaunted Amen.
A second he took. She departed. What then?
He courted and married a third — with Amen.
His joys and his sorrows were treble but then
His voice was deep bass as he sung out Amen.
His horn was exalted in blowing Amen,
He lost all his wind, at three-score-and-ten;
And here with three Wives he waits till again
The trumpet shall rouse him, to sing out Amen.'

Shovel, Lady Elizabeth (1659-1732). First married Sir John Narbrough, by whom she had one daughter, Elizabeth, who married Sir Thomas D'Aeth (see Knowlton—Narbrough), and two sons, John and James. After Narbrough died of fever at sea (see Knowlton—Narbrough) she married Sir Cloudesley Shovel by whom she had two daughters, Elizabeth and Ann. Elizabeth married Lord Romney; Ann married Robert Mansell (d.1723), who is also interred nearby. Her two sons by her first husband were serving aboard the ship *Association* with her second husband when all three perished. She is interred in St Paulinus Church, Crayford.

CROCKHAM HILL

Hill, Octavia (1838-1912). One of the Founders of the National Trust. A Victorian philanthropist and pioneer English social reformer who urged slum clearance in London. She was one of the first women to sit as a member of a Royal Commission. Her tomb is in Holy Trinity Church, Crockham Hill.

CUXTON

Marsham, Sir John (1602-1685). Writer, on Chronology. He wrote 'Diatriba Chronologica', 1649, concerning the Old Testament. He supported Charles I during the Civil War and after the King's defeat he retired to Whorne's Place, near Cuxton. For his support of the king he was knighted and in 1660 elected M.P. for Rochester. He had an extensive knowledge of history, languages and chronology and was said to have been the first to make Egyptian antiquities intelligible to the layman. His eldest son John commenced a history of England but did not publish it and also compiled a list of all the boroughs in England. Interred in St Michael's Church, Cuxton, where the eldest son John is also buried.

DARTFORD

Spielman, Sir John (d.1626). Founded the first paper mill in Kent after obtaining a licence from Elizabeth I to manufacture it at Dartford, 1588. His tomb with a figure of Sir John kneeling is in Holy Trinity Church, Dartford.

Trevithick, Richard (1771-1833). Locomotive Pioneer. Inventor. Engineer. He invented the first steam-propelled, passenger-carrying road vehicle, 1801, followed by a locomotive that ran on rails. His ideas were later developed by Stephenson. He also invented a pump for mines and a high-pressure steam engine. He worked prior to death at Hall's Engineering Works, Dartford. Interred in St Edmund's graveyard. Although he was buried in an unmarked grave it has been possible to approximate the site from contemporary records. A commemorative plaque has been placed as near as possible to the site of his grave in St Edmund's graveyard, now a public park, on East Hill.

DEAL

Parker, Edward Thornborough (1779-1801). Captain, R.N. One of Lord Nelson's Officers and a close friend, wounded in action off Boulogne, died at Deal on 27th September 1801, aged 22. Lord Nelson attended his funeral. Interred slightly to the south of the path that leads from St George's Church,

The grave of Captain Parker, one of Nelson's officers, at Lower Deal.
(Photograph by the author)

Lower Deal, to the south-west corner entrance, a few yards from Witherington's tomb (see below). Tomb inscription now illegible but a brass plate gives basic details. (See Eastry—Harvey)

Witherington, Henry (1778-1809). Expedition Victim. Lt., 63rd Regt. of Infantry. He took part in the disastrous Walcheren Expedition to secure that island, part of the Netherlands. The expedition force embarked from Deal on 30th July 1809 under the command of Lord Chatham (elder brother of Pitt), landed near Veere and seized it with Flushing and Middleburg. Witherington was one of the 7,000 who died of wounds or sickness (marsh fever) between landing and withdrawing in December 1809. Many other victims were also interred in the cemetery of St George's Church, Lower Deal. Witherington, who died 15th September 1809, aged 31, lies within a few yards of Captain Parker (see above) beneath a similar tomb on the wall side of the path that leads on the south side from the church through the cemetery to the south-west corner entrance. The inscription is almost illegible but a brass plate on it has readable details.

DEPTFORD

Marlowe, Christopher (1564-1593). Dramatist. Spy. Two of his principal plays are 'Dr Faustus' and 'Tamburlaine the Great'. Born at Canterbury and registered for birth in the parish of St George the Martyr, February 1564. A member of Lord Walsingham's 'Circle of Spies' working on the Continent and actually killed by members of that Company, June 1593, at a tavern in Deptford, supposedly during a 'brawl'. Interred in St Nicholas Churchyard, Deptford. (See Chislehurst—Thomas Walsingham; Linton—Mann)

DOVER

Churchill, Charles (1731-1764). Poet. Satirist. Interred in the old graveyard of St Martin's Church, Dover, near York Street, his grave being visited by Lord Byron. When the bypass road was built a Churchill grave was discovered in the old graveyard, but the position is now lost. On the south wall of St Mary's Church is a memorial tablet to him with lines from his 'Epistle to Hogarth'.

House, William (1879-1912). Victoria Cross Winner. Suicide. Private, 2nd Bn. Royal Berkshire Regt. He won his V.C. for rescuing a wounded sergeant under heavy fire on 2nd August 1900 in the Boer War. He committed suicide using his rifle to fire a high velocity bullet at very short range into his head shattering the skull, while in his room at the Shaft Barracks, Dover. The coroner recorded a verdict that the wound to the head he received winning the V.C., and later service in India, had contributed to House's suicide during temporary insanity. Interred, with full military honours, in St James's Cemetery, Dover.

McWheeney (or McWhiney), William (1837-1866). Victoria Cross Winner. Sgt., 1st Bn. 44th Regt. He won his V.C. in the Crimea for events on 20th October and 5th December 1854, and 18th June 1855. Interred in St James's Cemetery, Dover.

Wooden, Charles (1827-1876). Victoria Cross Winner. Sgt.-Major, later Lt., 17th Lancers. The only German to win the Victoria Cross, which he did in the Crimea on 25th October 1854, as a result of the Charge of the Light Brigade. He took part, with Surgeon James Mouat, V.C. (born Chatham, April 1815) in the rescue of a Lt.-Col. Morris and was instrumental in saving the officer's life. Interred in St James's Cemetery, Dover.

DYMCHURCH

Bedingfield, Timothy (1643-1693). Captain. Founder of an educational scholarship and a Christmas Charity at Dymchurch. On the south wall of the nave a memorial tablet to him and his wife Mary records that they gave their lands at Woodchurch and Liming 'towards Education, Maintenance and bringing up to Learning of such poor male children of such poor parents who do not receive parish relief or alms out of parish stock . . . and that such children be kept to learning and sent to one of the universities of Oxford or Cambridge if capable or put out to trade.' (See Cranbrook—Webster) The Bedingfield Charity also included '5/0 a peece unto two poor women of the parish to be paid on 25th December after they have received the Sacrament'. This is one of the very few examples of a Christmas charity in Kent benefactions, the majority being for Easter (see Lympne—Finch). The Bedingfield educational scholarships are still in existence. The memorial tablet records 'near this place lieth interred', so it is assumed he was probably interred outside in the old churchyard on the south side of St Peter & St Paul's Church, Dymchurch, where there are illegible headstones.

Rogers, Francis (d.1738). Riding Officer of His Majesty's Customs, stationed in Dymchurch. Served in the Army, fought in Spain, Flanders and Portugal, afterwards being a Riding Officer for 15 years, one of the many involved in the continual struggles against smugglers. Presumably he died a natural death! Numerous others were killed in battles and ambushes. Interred in the chancel, St Peter & St Paul's Church, Dymchurch.

In the churchyard there are tombstones marking the graves of other Riding Officers and Preventive Men, also those of office holders in the Ancient Corporations of the Lords of the Level and of the Liberty of Romney Marsh.

EAST FARLEIGH

Maxwell, Donald (1877-1936). Author. Artist. Tile Designer. Painted marine and landscape subjects in oil and water-colour. Official Artist to the Admiralty, 1914-18 War, with rank of Lieut. R.N.V.R. He accompanied the Prince of Wales in H.M.S. *Renown* and in India to prepare pictures of the Tour, and also illustrated the Prince of Wales' 'Eastern Book'. He wrote and illustrated travel and topographical books, particularly about Kent, such as 'A Detective in Kent', and 'Unknown Kent'. He designed ceramic tiles in co-operation with the Pembury Glazed Tile Co., and Doulton & Co., Lambeth, known as 'The Domesday Tiles'. It was intended that one tile would be prepared for each of the 350 or so places in Kent chosen, the tile depicting a local scene at that time in the 1930s. The tile series had only just been started when Maxwell died, but he had drawn and issued tiles for Linton, Wouldham, Westerham, Yalding, Guston, Chevening, Halling, Kemsing, Sheerness and Greenhithe. Two of his tiles are on an interior wall of Kemsing Church. One depicts the crossroads, Kemsing, the other the Pilgrim's Way. These were placed thereon by the vicar of Kemsing at the time who supported Maxwell's idea of every village having a tile recording a local view. Interred in St Mary's Churchyard, East Farleigh.

Hop Pickers' Memorial. In the churchyard of St Mary's Church, East Farleigh, near the War Memorial stands a wood cross with a canopy and the inscription 'In Memory of Forty-Three Strangers who died of Cholera. September 1849. R.I.P.'. 'Strangers' was the name used in the hop-growing areas of Kent for the people who came from East London annually for the hop picking. They often lived in harsh conditions near the hop gardens, in the 19th century, with poor sanitation and so cholera was easily spread. The original cross that had become dilapidated and rotten by 1984 has been removed and replaced by a varnished wood replica still bearing the inscription. (See Hadlow—Hartlake Bridge Disaster)

EAST MALLING

Thomlinson, Matthew (1617-1681). Barrister at the Inns of Court. Statesman. He fought with Cromwell's Parliamentarians. At the trial of Charles I he guarded the king and accompanied him to Westminster Hall and to his lodging afterwards, walking with the king to his execution in Whitehall, 1649, the king giving him his gold toothpick. At the Restoration of Charles II Thomlinson himself was probably saved from execution by his brother-in-law, Sir Thomas Twysden, a Royalist (see below). Interred in St James's Church, East Malling.

Twysden, Sir Thomas (1602-1683). One of the 'Regicide' Judges who had condemned Charles I to death. A Royalist, he married Parliamentarian Matthew Thomlinson's sister and probably saved Thomlinson from execution for escorting the king to his death. He was also Judge at the trials of John Bunyan, George Fox and wife Margaret Fell. His former home, Bradbourne, is now part of the East Malling Research Station. Interred in the Twysden Chapel, St James's Church, East Malling.

EAST PECKHAM

Twysden, Sir Roger (1597-1672). Royalist Pamphleteer. Antiquary. Brother of Judge Thomas Twysden (see East Malling). He supported Parliament until the Civil War then supported Charles I. He was imprisoned in a hulk on the Thames, then in Lambeth Palace. Here he wrote on antiquarian matters and when on bail kept a 'Journal' giving information on social life and public affairs and spoliation of his estate during the Parliamentary rule. He eventually won back his Roydon Hall and East Peckham estates. Interred in St Michael's Church, East Peckham.

EASTWELL

Hill, Allen (1776-1853). Park Keeper. In the churchyard of ruined St Mary's Church, Eastwell, is a gravestone placed there by George William, Earl of Winchelsea, to this man's memory and for his faithful service for 47 years as Park Keeper. The inscription is now almost illegible. (See Ashford—Waters, Kennington—Jones)

Plantagenet, Richard (1469-1550). Reputed natural son of Richard III. When 16 he witnessed the Battle of Bosworth, 1485, in which his father was killed. He thus became heir to the English throne, but wisely he fled knowing his father had many enemies and they would have also killed him. He is supposed to have arrived at Eastwell and worked as a bricklayer on the estate of Sir Thomas Moyle, who noticed Richard reading and writing when few labourers had these skills. Eventually he won Richard's confidence, so that he related his early life. Moyle, a Plantagenet sympathiser, gave him or allowed him to build a small house on the estate and provided for Richard until he died. Supposedly interred in a tomb in the chancel of ruined St Mary's Church, Eastwell, but this is open to conjecture. The parish register does, however, state Richard Plantagenet was buried at Eastwell on 22nd December 1550.

EASTRY

Harvey, John (1740-1794). Captain, R.N. From 1788 to 1792 commanded the *Arrogant*, a guardship for Sheerness. In 1793 he was appointed to the *Brunswick*, one of the Channel Fleet. At the Battle of the Glorious First of June the starboard anchor of the *Brunswick* hooked in the forechains of the French *Vengeur* and dragged the French ship along during the entire battle until the *Vengeur* eventually surrendered. The severely damaged *Brunswick* managed to reach Spithead. In the action Harvey's right hand was shattered by musket shot, then he was stunned by a heavy splinter hitting his back followed by a roundshot that smashed his right elbow. He died at Portsmouth, 30th June. He was younger brother of Admiral Sir Henry Harvey (d.1810, Walmer), who took part in the same battle. His own three sons were Admiral Sir Edward Harvey (d.1865) who was with his father on the *Brunswick* as a volunteer; Admiral Sir John Harvey (d.1837, Deal) and Henry Wise Harvey, the eldest son, who did not serve in the R.N. (though his two sons did). Harvey was a friend of Nelson (see Deal—Parker). Although there is a monument to him in Westminster Abbey he is interred in St Mary the Blessed Virgin Church, Eastry, where there is also a splendid marble relief of the battle by John Bacon on the north side of Eastry Church.

Nevinson, Thomas (d.1590). 'Provost Marshall and Scoutmaster of the East Partes of Kent and Captain of the Light Horses of the Lathe of St Augustine's'. Son of Christopher Nevynson, Lawyer of Adisham (d.1551). There is a sepulchral brass dated 1590 in the chancel, near the altar, to Thomas Nevynson and his wife Anne Theobald, in St Mary the Blessed Virgin Church, Eastry. After her first husband died Anne went to Faversham and married Edward Fagg. She died 21st November 1594, 'Mother of thirteen children by them both, Happy both in her Choice and Issue', but also apparently glad to return to Eastry Church to be interred with her first husband!

EDENBRIDGE

Timbs, John (1800/1-1875). Author. Editor. Journalist. Responsible for over 150 works which were wide ranging in subject, particularly in bringing little or unknown facts to the public, such as 'Knowledge for the People', 1831; 'Popular Errors Explained', 1841; 'Things Not Generally Known', 1856; 'Illustrated Year Book of Wonders', 1850. He also contributed to a large number of periodicals, but despite an enormous output he died in poverty in London. He was interred with a local family at Edenbridge who ran a school for boys, his sister having married the headmaster. Interred in St Peter & St Paul's Churchyard, Edenbridge.

The grave of Gipsy Chief Levi Boswell, and his wife Urania Boswell, 'Gipsy Lee', at Farnborough. (Photograph by courtesy of Kenneth Miller, Beckenham)

Sir John Pender's grave at Foots Cray. (Photograph by courtesy of Kenneth Miller, Beckenham)

EYNSFORD

Bosvile, Mary (1642-1659). A member of the Bosvile family who lived at Little Mote, Eynsford. Her epitaph is interesting. Interred in the south transept of St Martin's Church, Eynsford, where the floor inscription reads: 'Mistress Mary Bosvile, daughter of Sir Thomas Bosvile . . . who like a jewel taken out of a box was shewn to the world and put up again, January 18th, 1659, aged 17.' The memorial is also to 'her mother Lady Sarah Bosvile, wife to Colonel Richard Grimes who put off this her earthly tabernacle May 11, 1660'. She had married Grimes after her first husband's death in 1643.

Till, Elliott Downs (d.1917). Founder of Arbor Day in England, at Eynsford, the first village in this country to have the American practice. In the U.S.A., it was started by a settler in Nebraska in 1872 when one day a year was observed for tree planting, it eventually becoming a national custom. Several Arbor Days were held in Eynsford under Till's jurisdiction. The first was to commemorate Queen Victoria's Diamond Jubilee, 1897, when trees were planted so that the initial letters of the name of each tree when put together formed words and sentences. There were four sets. From the station to the village on the left-hand side could be spelt out a quotation from Browning: 'Grow old along with me, The best is yet to be.' Another in the meadow on the left-hand side of the village towards the mill from Little Mote Gate with trees planted in the year of Victoria's death, 1901, spelt a line from Tennyson: 'She wrought her people lasting good'. Around the school trees formed 'My son be wise' and around what is now the War Memorial four trees formed the word 'Love' with L for Lime, O for Olive, V for Veronica and E for Elm. On Arbor Day 1900, trees were planted in the village street to commemorate the relief of Mafeking, Ladysmith and Kimberley. A few of these Arbor Day trees still survive. Till also built the village hall at his own expense and in 1904 rebuilt the 'Harrow' public house, calling it the Castle Hotel. He was a tee-totaller and altered the hotel so that casual drinking only took place at the rear of the premises. The bar and tap rooms were separate from the hotel and entered through a door a distance away from the street. He also instructed the tenant in 1905 to display a notice that no ale, beer or other refreshment would be served on Sunday, except to visitors in the hotel, and only one alcoholic drink was to be served per day to each person. The brewery freeholders, anxious to sell more of their products, took Till to the High Court, but sur-prisingly Till won the case. So the brewers appealed and in the Court of Appeal Till lost. So came to an end his campaign for one man, one drink. Interred in St Martin's Churchyard, Eynsford, his headstone being situated halfway up the churchyard by the path.

EYTHORNE

Minet, Rev. John (1695-1771). Rector of Eythorne for almost 50 years, 1722-1771. He was also Chaplain of Dover Castle during this time but curiously his name continued in the Army Lists as holding the Chaplaincy until 1787. So who pocketed the dead Chaplain's salary during those 16 years — and did nobody at the Castle query why their Chaplain never held a service or attended any other religious function in that time? Interred in St Peter & St Paul's Church, Eythorne, where there is also a memorial tablet.

FARNBOROUGH

Boswell, Levi (1847-1924?). Gipsy Chief. It is difficult to read the year date as the stone has been broken and repaired (see next entry). Interred in St Giles' Churchyard, Farnborough.

Boswell, Urania. 'Gipsy Lee'. (1852-1933). Wife of Levi Boswell, the Gipsy (see above). Interred in St Giles' Churchyard, Farnborough. Also interred with them their son Percy Herbert Boswell (1872-1947) and Kenzie Boswell (1877-1949). Her funeral was a sensation in 1933 when some 15,000 people from all over the country arrived in Farnborough (then a village) to attend it.

Young, Thomas (1773-1829). Physicist. Egyptologist. Known as 'Phenom-enon Young' due to his wide range of knowledge of languages, mathematics, literature and science. Founder of 'physiological optics', he wrote 'On the Mechanism of the Eye' and carried out experiments on sound and light. He supported the wave theory of light, writing 'The Theory of Light and

Colours'. He was the first to use the terms 'energy' and 'labour expended' for power or force causing motion or action. He is probably best known today for his successful work on deciphering some of the hieroglyphic, enchorial and Greek characters of the Rosetta Stone discovered in Egypt in 1799. At the time of his death he was working on an Egyptian dictionary. Interred in St Giles' Church, Farnborough.

FARNINGHAM

Pounds, William (1723-1822). Died when 99, the oak board by the lychgate marking his grave having an appropriate quotation from the Bible: 'Thou shalt rise up before the hoary head and honour the face of the old man and fear thy God' – Lev. XIX, ver. 32. Interred in St Peter & St Paul's Churchyard, Farningham.

Roper, Anthony (buried August 1597). Son of Margaret Roper, eldest daughter of Sir Thomas More, being the latter's grandson and Lord of the Manor of Farningham. He founded the Roper Charity. Interred with his wife Anne Roper in the chancel of St Peter & St Paul's Church, Farningham, where there is also an alabaster monument on the north wall to the Roper family with details and kneeling figures. (See Canterbury; Lynsted—Roper family)

In the churchyard of St Peter & St Paul's Church, Farningham, sited between the church and vicarage, is a mausoleum that may possibly be an early example of the work of John Nash, the Regency architect and nephew of Thomas Nash. The wall inscription reads: 'This Mausoleum was begun by Thomas Nash, Esq., Merchant, Citizen of London and one of His Majesty's Justices of the Peace for the counties of Kent and Surrey who died at Paris April 7th, 1778, and whose Remains are here deposited and Finished by his Executors for a Burying Place for himself and Family.' Inside the mausoleum from below ground level to rooftop height are bricked up against the walls the remains of Thomas Nash and numerous relatives. Some seventy or so years ago there used to be a game among Farningham schoolgirls who tried to throw a pin through the opening immediately above the inscription. Having thrown the pin they would run round the mausoleum expecting the Devil to look out if they had made an accurate throw. There is no record of any girls ever succeeding in causing the Devil to appear! (See Rainham—Chambers and Devil)

FAVERSHAM

Stephen (King of England 1135-1154). Usurped the Crown from his cousin Matilda, the rightful heir. Survived while sustained by the Church but when he lost this support in 1139 civil war began between Matilda's forces and his own. During excavations in the Royal Chapel of Faversham Abbey in 1965 two vaults were exposed in which Stephen and Matilda (his wife, not his cousin) had been interred. The Royal Chapel was a large mausoleum, measuring 7 feet by 7 feet, and would have contained coffins with their bodies, but no trace of either was discovered. It is likely these vaults remained intact until the Dissolution of the monasteries, then sometime shortly after 1538 they were robbed. Thomas Southouse, Snr (d.1676), author of a Survey of Faversham Monastery, wrote 'when for the gain of the lead wherein this King's body was incoffined his sacred remains were dislodged and thrown into the neighbouring river' (the Ospringe/Faversham 'nailbourne'). In the Trinity Chapel of nearby St Mary of Charity Parish Church, Faversham, is a tomb wherein the bones of Stephen and wife Matilda were reputed to be interred. The excavation did not disprove the comment of Southouse nor the local tradition.

Victims of the Explosion at the Cotton Powder Company's Gunpowder Factory, Uplees, Faversham. This took place on 2nd April 1916, due to an accidental fire, cause unknown, as a result of which 106 persons died. A mass grave and memorial for 60 of the victims is in Faversham Cemetery, Love Lane, but only 34 of these could, at the time of the funeral on 6th April 1916, be definitely recorded by name. Of those who died all but five, who were in the military guard, were civilian employees. Other victims were interred elsewhere.

FOLKESTONE

Calverley, Charles Stuart (1831-1884). Scholar. Humorous Poet. Wit. Translator. Known as the 'Prince of Parodists'. He began as a barrister after being called to the Bar, 1865, but a fall while ice skating in the winter 1866-67, in which the injury was neglected until it became apparent he had suffered severe brain concussion, ended his brilliant career in the law. His later years were spent as an invalid writing, as he had done early in life. His books include 'Verses & Translations', 1862; 'Theocritus Translated into English Verse', 1869 and 'Fly Leaves', 1872. Interred in Cheriton Road Cemetery, Folkestone.

Commerell, John Edmund (1829-1901). Victoria Cross Winner. Commander (later Admiral of the Fleet) R.N. Won his V.C. on 11th October 1855, while serving on H.M.S. *Weser* in the Crimean War. Interred in Cheriton Road Cemetery, Folkestone.

Crowe, Catherine (1790-1872). Novelist. Author of books and articles on the supernatural. Writer of children's fiction. Tract Writer. Translator. A 'pioneer of novels of the domestic interior'. Her interests included phrenology, spiritualism, physiology (now psychology) and she investigated the supernatural. Her literary output, fiction and non-fiction, was tremendous, her mostly successful novels being 'Susan Hopley', 1841 and 'Linny Lockwood', 1853. Some of her stories have Kentish backgrounds. Other works included 'The Night Side of Nature or Ghosts and Ghost Seers', 1848, concerned with the psychic analysis of ghost appearances; 'Ghosts and Family Legends', 1858; 'Spiritualism and the Age We Live In', 1859. Her 5-Act Drama, 'The Cruel Kindness', was performed in London, June 1853. She died at Sandgate Road, Folkestone, of 'natural decay' and was interred in Cheriton Road Cemetery, Folkestone.

Eanswythe, Abbess (d.640? possibly aged 26). Grand-daughter of King Ethelbert, daughter of Eadbald, who founded a nunnery church for her near Folkestone. Erosion of the coast caused the destruction of this church in which her remains had been interred, but these had been transferred to another church, St Peter & St Paul's, just before the inundation. The sea eventually eroded the coast further and this church in turn was destroyed by falling into the sea. In 1138 William d'Averanches, Lord of the Manor of Folkestone had built the present church and into this new building the remains were again translated just in time. The remains were enshrined on 12th September, still observed as St Eanswythe's Day. In 1535 on the orders of Henry VIII the shrine was destroyed. It seemed the remains of Eanswythe were lost. In 1885 workmen discovered a niche plastered over in the north wall. In it stood a lead coffer, 14 inches long, 9 inches wide and 8 inches high, containing portions of limbs, skull, ribs, hands, feet, teeth, a jawbone, examined by an anatomist in 1980 and identified as belonging to a young woman aged 18 to 25, about 5 feet 4 inches tall, supporting the tradition that they are the bones of St Eanswythe which at their last translation probably broke to pieces, she having been dead 500 years. It confirmed also a belief through the centuries that the bones had been gathered together and secreted somewhere in the church at the destruction of the shrine. The position near the high altar indicates they were given a place of honour and so were of no ordinary person. They were returned to the niche still in their coffer and a brass grille was placed in front of them. This lies behind a locked, engraved brass door, in the north wall of St Mary & St Eanswythe's Church, Folkestone.

Fitzgerald, Charles Egerton (1830-1898). Doctor, who practised for many years in Folkestone and did much to bring it into national prominence as a health giving resort. Founder and President of the Folkestone Natural History Society. Interred in Cheriton Road Cemetery, Folkestone.

Kerr, William Alexander (1831-1919). Victoria Cross Winner. Lt. (later Capt.) 24th Bombay Native Infantry, Indian Army. Won his V.C. on 10th July 1857, during the Indian Mutiny. Interred in Cheriton Road Cemetery, Folkestone.

Lindon, Herbert (d.1909). Son of John Keats' love, Fanny Brawne, who later married to become Mrs Louis Lindon. Herbert Lindon lived at 4 Augusta Gardens, Folkestone, from 1889-98/9, then moved to live with his wife at 19 Trinity Gardens until he died. Interred in Cheriton Road Cemetery, Folkestone.

Rogers, Rebecca (1645-1689). Who she was is not known but the inscription on her headstone has gained much prominence. Its wording suggests that in life she may have campaigned against the hated chimney tax. It reads:

'A house she hath, its made of such good fashion
The tenant ne'er shall pay for reparation,
Nor will her landlord ever raise her rent,
Or turn her out of doors for non-payment.
From chimney money, too, this cell is free,
Of such a house who would not tenant be?'

Originally sited under the east window of the north chapel in the churchyard, some years ago the stone was brought inside to preserve it and it is now in the library corner of St Mary & St Eanswythe Church, Folkestone. (See Cheriton—Chisman)

Walker, Sir Mark (1827-1902). Victoria Cross Winner. Lt. (later General), 1st Bn., 30th Regt. He won his V.C. at Inkerman, Crimea, on 5th November 1854 and was dangerously wounded at the Siege of Sebastopol but recovered to take part in the China Campaign, 1860. Interred in Cheriton Road Cemetery, Folkestone.

Faulkner Wives' Oven Grave. On the west side of St Mary & St Eanswythe's Churchyard, Folkestone, is an **'oven grave'** or vault containing two interments: Fanny Faulkner (d.1853) and Emily Faulkner (d.1862), the wives of a Francis Faulkner. The curve of the mound is made of bricks, reminiscent of the larger **'oven graves'** at Bethersden and Smarden. Possibly in the past this vault was also covered with earth and grass. (See Bethersden, Smarden—oven graves)

FOOTS CRAY

Pender, Sir John (1816-1895). Pioneer of Submarine Telegraphy. One of the original 345 contributors of £1,000 each towards the cost of the necessary experiments, he was made a director of the Atlantic Cable Company, 1856. He shared the disappointment and frustration of all attempts for the scheme for eight years. The breaking of the cable in 1865 in mid-ocean during the historic voyage of the *Great Eastern* finally ruined the Atlantic Cable Company. He was joint founder of the Anglo-American Company, 1865, with plans for a new, stronger cable to be made by the Gutta Percha Company and another company, the Glass Elder Company. They wanted guarantees of payment so Pender pledged his personal fortune of £250,000. The two firms combined to form the Telegraph Construction & Maintenance Company, of which he was chairman. The new cable was successfully laid in 1866 and the broken cable recovered. He was later involved in electric lighting for London as chairman of the Metropolitan Electric Supply Company. Interred with his wife Emma in All Saints Churchyard, Foots Cray, the grave marked by a large cross.

The 'oven grave' or vault of the Faulkner Wives in St Mary and St Eanswythe's Churchyard, Folkestone.   (Photograph by the author)

The table tomb of John Timbs at Edenbridge.
(Photograph by courtesy of Alan Dell, Edenbridge)

56

FORDCOMBE

Hardinge, Sir Arthur Edward (1828-1892). General. Served in the First Sikh War, also at the battles of Moodkee, Sobraon and Ferozeshah. Served in the Crimea, at the battles of Alma, Balaclava and Inkerman, and at the fall of Sebastopol. Later Equerry to Prince Albert and on his death to Queen Victoria. Having survived such events in war he died from injuries received in a carriage accident at Weymouth. Interred at St Peter's Church, Fordcombe.

Hardinge, Charles Stewart, 2nd Viscount Hardinge (1822-1894). Eldest son of 1st Viscount, Henry Hardinge. Although intended for a career in the army an accident as a boy compelled him to have an artificial leg and ended these hopes. So he became private secretary to his father in India when the latter was Governor-General. He was a skilled watercolour artist and in India painted portraits of Sikh chieftains and the then almost unknown Kashmir scenery that he visited. Interred in St Peter's Church, Fordcombe.

Hardinge, Sir Henry, 1st Viscount Hardinge of Lohore (1785-1856). Served in the army at the battles of Vimeira and Corunna, being at the side of Sir John Moore when the latter received his fatal injuries. He was the British Military Commissioner at Blucher's headquarters. While sketching near the Prussian positions, at Ligny during the battle of Quatre Bras, 1815, a stone thrown up by a bursting shell smashed his left hand. It had to be amputated at once and so he missed the Battle of Waterloo, but a fortnight after the amputation he returned to Blucher's headquarters. For his various duties he was presented with a sword of honour by Wellington, and he was Secretary for War, 1828-1830, in the latter's Government. He was also the Duke's second when the Duke fought a duel with Lord Winchilsea. Governor-General of India, 1844-1848, he made numerous beneficial reforms, founded schools and was involved in starting the Indian Railway system. He died at South Park, Tunbridge Wells, and was interred in St Peter's Church, Fordcombe, the foundation stone of which he had laid on his return from India and for which he had contributed the greater part of the cost.

FORDWICH

Harris (?), Mistress (d.1570). A brass in the floor of St Mary the Virgin's Church, Fordwich, commemorates 'The wife of the Queenes Maiestes fruiterer'. He was Richard Harris, erroneously credited with introducing the cultivated cherry to Kent. He *was* involved in its cultivation in the Teynham area and is also supposedly interred in Fordwich Church, the case for this being strong. The Harris family had been and still was then involved with the Cinque Ports, of which Fordwich was one member. The Cinque Ports cesse (a tax or assessment) for Shipping of Queen Elizabeth refers to a William Harris, an ancestor of Richard, 'cessed at 5 shillings'. This association adds strength to the possibility that Richard Harris is therein, perhaps with his wife.

GILLINGHAM

Bell, David (1845-1920). Victoria Cross Winner. Private, 2nd Bn., 24th Regt. His V.C. was not awarded for bravery in action against a wartime enemy but for bravery at sea and in rescuing comrades from cannibals, on 7th May 1867. From the vessel *Assam Valley* a party of soldiers and sailors went ashore to investigate Little Andaman Island, Bay of Bengal. They did not return. A second party of 17 men and 1 officer was sent to find them and when they also did not return Bell was in the third party that went in search of the others. The skulls of the first party were found on the shore, the bodies having been eaten by cannibals, while the second group were discovered trapped by the cannibals whom they were trying to keep at bay. The third group rescued their trapped comrades and, pursued by arrow-firing and spear-throwing natives, managed to get to their boat and over the raging surf to the ship. It was during this action that the heroism of Bell and four others was rewarded with the V.C. Interred in Woodlands Cemetery, Woodlands Road, Gillingham. Another V.C. winner from the 2nd Bn. 24th Regt. attended Bell's funeral. He was Private John Williams (1857-1933) who won his V.C. at Rorke's Drift, in the Zulu War, 1879. (See Beckenham—Bourne)

Dobson, Claude Congreve (1885-1940). Victoria Cross Winner. Commander (later Rear-Admiral), R.N., D.S.O. He was awarded the V.C. for his part in the attack on the Russian Fleet, Krondstadt Harbour, on 18th August 1919, while commanding H.M. Coastal Motor Boat 31. Interred in Woodlands Cemetery, Woodlands Road, Gillingham. (See entry below and other V.C. winners at Shorncliffe, Folkestone, etc.)

Esmonde, Eugene (1909-1942). Victoria Cross Winner. Lt-Cmdr., R.N., D.S.O. Leader of the six Swordfish biplanes from Manston that attacked the German capital ships *Scharnhorst, Gneisenau* and *Prinz Eigen* on 12th February 1942, during their daylight 'Channel dash' to their home ports. Only three of the 18 crew members of six aircraft survived. Six days later Esmonde's body was washed ashore in the Medway estuary. He was the first naval officer, Fleet Air Arm, to be awarded the V.C. on the recommendation of an R.A.F. officer, the C.O. of Manston. Interred in Grave 187 in the Roman Catholic section, Woodlands Cemetery, Woodlands Road, Gillingham. (See Beckenham—Evans; Canterbury—Byrne; and other V.C. winners)

Millions, Mr Robert (1759-1830). Master, R.N. the word Mr on the headstone refers to his title from his seafaring profession. This surnamed grave was the origin of a local joke. When a passer-by enquired of the sexton one day how many were buried in the churchyard he replied 'There is millions buried in Gillingham Churchyard'. Interred at the end of the fifth row back, near the old yew tree, in the section reserved as a memorial garden for cremation remains opposite the main tower entrance to St Mary Magdalene's Church, Gillingham.

Victims of the 'Firemen's Wedding' Fire Disaster. At the Gillingham Park Fete, on 11th July 1929, a specially built, three-storey, forty-foot high 'house' of matchboarding with wood doors and floors had been constructed following the practice of the previous twenty years. It was used to demonstrate the prowess of Gillingham Fire Brigade in dousing a fire. The performance began with a 'mock wedding' party with 'wedding guests' portrayed by firemen, sea cadets and boy scouts, including a 'bride', 'groom' and 'auntie', the latter played by a naval petty officer. The party amused the crowd and then gathered in the 'house', red flares were lit to simulate fire and fire engines would rush to the 'rescue'. After all had been 'rescued' the 'house' would be set alight and tackled by firemen. On this occasion flames reputedly started in some shavings on the ground floor (one witness said the second storey) and the towerlike 'house', acting like a chimney, was soon an inferno trapping the victims on the upper storey. Nine boys and six men died from burns, including Petty Officer John Nutton — 'auntie', Fireman Arthur Tabrett — 'groom' and Fireman Arthur Worrall — 'bride'. The inquest jury recorded a verdict of 'death by misadventure'. As a result all similar displays were banned by the Home Office. A mass funeral of the victims was held on Wednesday 17th July, the draped coffins being carried on ten fire appliances, and five naval gun carriages. The victims were interred in a row of graves facing the naval section in Woodlands Cemetery, Woodlands Road, Gillingham.

Royal Marine Cadets Disaster, Dock Road, Chatham, 1951. Nineteen of those killed when a bus ran into a column of cadets were interred in the main naval section and another three in the Roman Catholic area of the naval section, Woodlands Cemetery, Woodlands Road, Gillingham, in December 1951. Another victim, James Trigg, was interred in St Margaret's Churchyard, Rainham.

Naval Victims, First World War. Victims of the H.M.S. *Bulwark* battleship explosion, November 1914; the *Princess Irene* minelayer explosion, May 1915; and the air raid on the Royal Naval Barracks, Chatham, 1917 are also interred in the naval section of Woodlands Cemetery, Woodlands Road, Gillingham.

GODMERSHAM

Austen, Edward (1768-1852). Third brother of Jane Austen. He inherited Godmersham Park and property from Thomas Knight, so changed his name to Knight. His sisters, Jane and Cassandra Austen, often visited him here and worshipped in the church, where there is a memorial on the north wall of the nave. Interred in the family vault in St Lawrence the Martyr's Church, Godmersham.

Mun, Rev. Richard (1639-1682). Vicar of Godmersham. His epitaph on the north wall of the nave of Godmersham Church, near the pulpit, has interesting examples of the earlier form of spelling in inscriptions. One example is Ientry for Gentry; I here is really our J. 'Neare this place in hope of a Ioyfull resurrection resteth ye body of Richard Mun, Mr. etc.' There follows a very long inscription in Roman capitals and lower case lettering which crowds much text into a small space. The black slate memorial has a shield of arms of the Mun family on the left, in pale (side by side with) those of the Hopkins family of his wife. This is the correct way of showing the arms of a man and his wife. Interred in St Lawrence the Martyr's Church, Godmersham.

Sackree, Susanna (1761-1851). Servant Nurse at Godmersham Park for the Knight (Austen) family for almost sixty years. In a number of Jane Austen's letters to her sister Cassandra she is referred to in affectionate terms. Interred in St Lawrence the Martyr's Churchyard, Godmersham. On the exterior of the church, on the north-east buttress, there is a memorial to her with almost illegible lettering. On this at her own request the following inscription was cut: 'Flee from evil and to the thing that is good,/For the Lord loves the thing that is good./Keep innocency and take heed unto the thing that is right for that shall bring a man peace at the last./My dearest friends I leave behind/Who were to me so good and kind/The Lord I hope will all them bless/And my poor soul will be at rest.' (See Kennington—Jones)

GOUDHURST

Culpeper (Colepepper), Sir Alexander (d.1537). The near-lifesized painted effigies of him and his wife, Dame Constance, are carved in wood, rare for such figures, and dated 1537, when he died. In the south aisle of St Mary's Church, Goudhurst.

Culpeper (Colepepper), Sir Alexander (d.1599). Knighted by Queen Elizabeth I whom he entertained at his house at Bedgebury during her Kent Progress, 1573. The alabaster monument in the Bedgebury Chapel, St Mary's Church, Goudhurst, was erected by his son, Sir Anthony, in 1608 and is by Epiphanus Evesham.

Fegan, James William Condell (1852-1925). Founder of Homes for Boys, Deptford, 1870; Greenwich, 1879; Southwark, 1882 and his first orphanage, Ramsgate, 1883. Founder of Mr. Fegan's Homes, Goudhurst, where several farms using Canadian farming equipment, Canadian barns and other buildings Canadian-style were used to train boys who were then sent to Canada in groups of fifty to start a new life on farms there. Mary, his wife, (1865-1943), became President of the Homes after his death. She was killed by a German bomb which fell on her retirement home, October, 1943. Both interred in St Mary's Churchyard, Goudhurst.

Freeman, Ann (d.1798). Smallpox Inoculation Victim. The inscription on her gravestone in St Mary's Churchyard, Goudhurst, states: 'Ann, daughter of William and Phoebe Freeman, who died with the Enoculation of the Small Pox aged 11'. Other smallpox victims are Hothfield—Stanford; Pluckley—Nepecker; Sundridge—Clavell.

GRAVENEY

Keys, Nelson Waite ('Bunch') (1887-1939). Actor. Character Comedian. Film Star. First appearance on stage 1906. Made 21 short and full length films. First, a short, 'Drowsy Dick's Dream', 1909; last two, full-length 'Wake Up Famous' and 'Knights For A Day', 1937. His biography, 'Bunch', was published 1941. Interred on west side of All Saints' Churchyard, close to tower, Graveney. (See Margate—Fuller)

GRAVESEND (GRAVESHAM)

Freeman, Richard Austin (1862-1943). Novelist. Physician. Author of articles and books on medical subjects. In 1907 published 'The Red Thumb Mark', his first novel in which 'Dr. John Thorndyke', as a medico-legal consultant and detective scientifically investigated and solved criminal and other cases. He wrote 21 novels and 40 short stories using 'Thorndyke'. Interred in Milton & Gravesend Municipal Cemetery, Gravesham.

Pocahontas, Princess (Mrs. John Rolfe) (1595-1617). Daughter of Powhattan, over-chief of the Indian tribes in Virginia. Interceded with her father and saved the life of Captain John Smith, leader of the settlers in 1607, and then married John Rolfe, 1613, the first cultivator of tobacco in Virginia. On marriage she became a Christian and took the name of Rebecca. In 1616 came to London with her husband and was a great favourite at court, especially with Queen Anne, wife of James I. Died aboard ship at Gravesend, either of consumption or smallpox, shortly before she was due to return to Virginia with her husband and son. There is some confusion about her burial place. According to the church register 'Rebecca Rolf.. a Virginian borne lady was buried in ye chauncell' of St George's Church, Gravesend, but in 1907 during excavations in the churchyard near to the church a skeleton was discovered that was claimed to be that of a young female Indian, whether Pocahontas or not is uncertain. The original St George's Church was burnt down in 1727 and rebuilt in 1731 when it is possible the area of the church's foundations may have been altered. Thus Pocahontas may be buried either within the church or in the churchyard — or is she elsewhere? A successful American application was made to the Home Office in 1923 to excavate for the remains of Pocahontas in the church and, when found, to return them to the USA. Several graves were opened that were known to have been in the church when it burnt down in the 18th century. Sir Arthur Keith, the anthropologist, confirmed that her bones were not among the reinterred remains.

Fifty bodies were exhumed in the churchyard but hers was not among them and they were reinterred. A skull was found that did approximate to a Red Indian type but proof was not conclusive. Portions of over a hundred skeletons were found beneath rubbish in a 19th century table tomb probably used as a depository when the bones were found during gravedigging in the churchyard. No Indian remains were among these and they were also reinterred. This work caused much indignation and protests among people in Gravesend. The question is: Was she ever interred in St George's Church or Churchyard? In June, 1923, a letter was published in the 'Daily Mail' from a reader stating that his grandfather had told him Pocahontas was not interred at St George's but instead was in the old church of St Mary that no longer exists. Two days later another letter was printed from a different reader who, when the reader was six years old, had been taken by her grandmother to a spot marked by a memorial tablet in the ancient burial ground of Gravesend partly bounded by Windmill Street and Wrotham Road and surrounded by a seven foot high wall. The grandmother told the reader that in the burial ground were interred all those who died aboard ship off Gravesend and foreigners, too, as it was thought unseemly to bury them in the parish churchyard among the generations of local people. (See Littlebourne—Wyman)

GREAT CHART

Leet, William Knox (1833-1898). Major-General, Prince Albert's Somerset-shire Light Infantry. He won the Victoria Cross 'for his gallant conduct on March 28th 1879, in rescuing from the Zulus Lt. A.M. Smith, of the Frontier Light Horse, during the retreat from Inhlobana Mountain. Lt. Smith, while on foot, his horse having been shot, was closely pursued by the Zulus and would have been killed had not Major Leet taken him upon his horse and rode with him, under a hail of assegais and rifle fire of the enemy, to a place of safety.' Died at Ashford, interred in St Mary the Virgin's Churchyard, Great Chart.

Toke, Nicholas (1588-1680). 'The Captain'. Member of the family which held Great Chart and Godinton Manors. He married five times and is supposed to have been on his way to London in January 1680, aged 93, to find a sixth wife when he died! Interred in the Toke family vault in St Mary the Virgin's Church, Great Chart. In the floor of the north chapel Nicholas Toke is depicted with his five wives and three kneeling daughters.

GROOMBRIDGE

Oswell, William Cotton (1818-1893). African Explorer. Known as 'The Nimrod of South Africa'. A memorial tablet over the south door was placed there by the Royal Geographical Society in recognition of his discovery of Lake Ngami, 1849, with his friend and companion, Dr Livingstone. He was with him too at the discovery of the Zambesi, 1851. The Straight-Horned Rhinoceros was named Oswellii after him. During the Crimean War he carried secret service money alone, after his escort deserted, from Lord Raglan to Sir Linton Simmons. Interred in St John's Church, Groombridge.

Packer, Philip (1618-1686). Founder Member of the Royal Society. Barrister in the Middle Temple. A friend of John Evelyn, the Diarist and Arboriculturist, who visited him at Groombridge and helped plan the gardens. He was third son of John Packer (1570-1649), Clerk of the Privy Seal, who, in 1625, rebuilt Groombridge Chapel after purchasing the moated manor, Groombridge Place. In the north side of the chancel over the priest's door of St John's Church, Groombridge, is a deep niche with the monument to Philip Packer, the figure having the legs crossed and head resting on one shoulder, as if the neck is broken. There is a tradition that Packer was found dead in this position in an arbour in the garden of the Place. Interred, as was his father, in a vault in the chancel of St John the Apostle's Chapel, Groombridge.

HADLOW

May, Walter (d.1823). Built Hadlow Castle, commencing in the late 1780s and completing it to his plans in 1803. He was interred in a tomb in St Mary's Churchyard, Hadlow, but later exhumed and re-interred in the mausoleum built for his son Walter Barton May (which see). In the middle aisle of the nave of the church is the grave, covered by a flat stone, of Thomas May (d.1714), an ancestor of the May family.

May, Walter Barton (1783-1855). Son of Walter May. About 1838 he started to build the 170 feet high Tower adjoining the Castle. In 1840 a lantern was added which makes it different from other towers on which the design was based. It is known locally as 'May's Folly'. Local legend says he built it to spy on his wife Mary Porter who had left him in 1836 and was living at her family home, Fishall, Hadlow, though other accounts state that he built it so that he could see the sea from its summit. The main tomb for the May family is the mausoleum built for his son Walter Barton May (see below). In the middle Churchyard, Hadlow. The mausoleum was built in 1855 at a cost of £135.11s. 5d, to contain Walter Barton May, but his father and mother were re-interred there and now there are eight members of the family and relatives within.

The Hartlake Bridge Disaster Victims, Hadlow. On 20th October 1853, hop picking was taking place in gardens adjoining the Medway at Hadlow when, due to heavy rain, the low-lying gardens on the Hadlow side became flooded and picking impossible. It was decided by the farmer, a Mr. Cox of Thomson's Farm, Golden Green, to move the pickers to hop gardens on the other side of the river above the flood level. Another version states that the picking had ended and transport was sent to take the pickers to Tudeley, where they were camping, until the river level dropped. Two waggons arrived for the pickers. One was loaded and the pickers reached the other side of the river safely. On to the second waggon between thirty and forty pickers, including the waggoner and bailiff, climbed and set off. When they reached Hartlake Bridge, a wooden structure 9 feet 3 inches wide by 42 feet long with a slope of 1 in 5 each side, it was discovered that the river had risen even higher and was rushing over the level of the bridge. The two horses hauling the waggon were tandem fashion, one in front of the other, the fore-horse also carrying a labourer. The bailiff, waggoner and labourer apparently thought it safe to cross. When in the centre of the bridge it seems the fore-horse stumbled so the rear-horse in the shafts turned to the right and forced the waggon against the centre post of the wooden side which, like the rest of the posts and rails, was rotten and snapped under the pressure. The water carried the waggon over the side, capsizing it as it fell. The bailiff and waggoner managed to save themselves by jumping off the front of the waggon on to the bridge, but those in the waggon fell into the swollen river, were carried away and the majority drowned, thirty men, women and children losing their lives. The two horses saved themselves as the shafts had broken off as the waggon fell. Several of the people were washed into trees overhanging the river and were rescued. The youngest victim was Catherine Herne, aged 2, the oldest, Samuel Leatherland, aged 59. In one instance a boy survived, but his mother, father and sisters were drowned. An inquest was held on 22nd October at the 'Bell' Inn, Hadlow, and an accidental death verdict given on the victims, with a rider that the Medway Navigation Company should rebuild the bridge in stone with higher sides. The Company also paid £63 12s. 5d. for the costs of the victims' interment and monument. Interments took place over a period from 24th October to 14th November, probably due to the times when the bodies were recovered. For several years following the disaster a wreath of hops was thrown from the new bridge into the river every hop picking season and a short memorial service was held but this is now discontinued. The monument marking the interment place of the victims stands in the south-east corner of St Mary's Churchyard, Hadlow. It has a pyramid-like summit and bears the names of all the victims although some are now illegible. Originally there were railings around it but apparently these were removed in the Second World War. (See East Farleigh—Hop Pickers' Memorial)

HARBLEDOWN

Anderson, William (d.1835?/7?). Suicide. Igglesden, in Vol. XXIX of his 'A Saunter Through Kent' — Harbledown, tells of 'a gravestone in the south corner of St Nicholas Churchyard with the name Anderson engraved on it, Anderson being a remarkably religious type of man and in his capacity of sexton considered it his duty always to visit the church at midnight and at last in a fit of madness he hanged himself in the tower.' There are two Anderson graves, both with the Christian name William, on the east side of the church chancel close to the side path under some yew trees. The most likely is the headstone to William Anderson which reads: 'Charity. Covereth All Things, Believeth All Things, Hopeth All Things, Endureth All Things. William

Anderson. Fifteen Years Clerk of this Parish, died June? 1837 or 1857 (the 3 or 5 is almost illegible), aged 31 or 51 (again the 3 or 5 is very indistinct). He had lived beloved and respected by all who knew him and by none more than his sorrowing rector who inscribed this stone to the memory of a zealous officer and attached friend.' The last three lines cannot be seen fully as they are behind the footstone placed at a later date against the headstone. The headstone inscription faces east away from the church, (as does Smarden—Wilmot), whereas the other inscriptions nearby face west. The other William Anderson stone is sited facing west in the same row a few feet to the north, and is inscribed 'William Anderson died January ? 1802, aged 71. Mary, wife of the above died ? 1817, aged 79, also Thomas, Grandson of above who died ? 1819 aged 10'. It would seem from this that the older William Anderson was the grandfather of the suicide William Anderson and Thomas was younger brother of the suicide William Anderson if the latter died in 1837 aged 31. It is often thought suicides were interred on the north, coldest side of the churchyard, sometimes in unconsecrated ground, as a 'punishment' for the 'sin' of taking one's life. Anderson's interment site confounds this belief. Perhaps the sorrowing vicar decided Anderson deserved better, being mentally ill, so had him interred on the east side and even apparently paid for the inscribed headstone. The only suggestion of a 'punishment' is that the wording faces east, away from the church, while neighbouring headstone inscriptions face west and the church. No-one can know now what really lay behind this tragedy. (See High Halden; Ickham-de Baa; Smarden—Wilmot)

HARRIETSHAM

Stede, William (d.1574). Yeoman, Stede Street. A descendant, through his eldest daughter Susannah (d.1603, interred in the Stede Chapel, Harrietsham Church) and her daughter Catherine (interred Hollingbourne 1599), was Gulielma Maria Springate (1644-1693) who in 1672 became the wife of William Penn, Quaker founder of Pennsylvania. His son, Sir William Stede (1565?-1620, interred in the Stede Chapel, Harrietsham Church), was builder of Stede Hill (home of Robert H. Goodsall, author—historian). William Stede, the father, was interred in a large, inscribed altar tomb in the Stede Chapel, in St John the Baptist's Church, Harrietsham. Another descendant was Edwyn Stede (1700-1735), the 'Father of Kent Cricket', and first Kent County player of whom there is a record. He had his own Club, and sponsored games, Kent v London, Surrey, etc., playing against sides led by the Prince of Wales and other nobility. Edwyn is believed to have died at Boxley.

HARTLIP

Coppin, Mary (d.1636, aged 24). Died in 'child-bed'. Daughter of Edward Osborne. The Osbornes were land and property owners in the area, a number of them being interred in the church or commemorated therein. The monument to Mary in the north chapel has the inscription: 'Having so with wisdom crowned her days, That time could not have added to her praise, She's called to Heaven with angels, there to sing, The joyful tidings which this day did bring'. Interred in St Michael & All Angels Church, Hartlip. Across the fields from Hartlip, and almost within sight, stands Stockbury Church, where another childbirth fatality is interred in the chancel. (See Stockbury— Ruffin)

HAWKHURST

Kilburne, Richard (1605-1678). Kentish Topographer. Solicitor in Chancery. J.P. for Kent. During the Commonwealth he celebrated marriages at Hawkhurst without sacred rites, but is thought to have married only two couples in this way. In 1657 published 'A Brief Survey of the County of Kent', listing parish names, dedications of churches and market and fair days. In 1659 published his 'larger survey' 'A Topographic or Survey of the County of Kent with historicall and other matters touching the same, etc.', which is not very comprehensive but contains much about Hawkhurst where Kilburne lived on his Fowlers estate. Interred in the north chapel of St Laurence's Church, Hawkhurst, where there is a flat memorial stone.

HAWKINGE

Feist, Nellie (1867-1917). One of the victims killed in an air raid by German Gotha bombers on Folkestone, 25th May 1917, aged 50, together with her grandson, Stanley Albert Feist, aged 5 years. James McCudden (See Chatham—McCudden) while returning to France reputedly took an ineffective part in the air battle against the Gothas. Interred in St Michael's Churchyard, Hawkinge. (See Gillingham)

HAYES

Panis, John (d.1763). Infant. The puzzling epitaph states: 'In memory of John Panis, of the Tribe of Panis in North America, who died 14th January 1763, aged Nine Years'. Interred in St Mary's Churchyard, Hayes.

HERNE BAY

Cooper, William Sidney (1854-1927). Landscape Artist. Great-nephew of Thomas Sidney Cooper, R.A. Painted local rural scenes, one being 'The Bridge at Fordwich'. Interred in Eddington Cemetery, Canterbury Road, on the outskirts of Herne Bay.

HERNHILL

Tom, John Nichols (alias 'Sir William Percy Honeywood Courtenay', 'The New Messiah', 'Mad Tom') (1799-1838). Attempted to stand as M.P. for Canterbury, then Thanet, but was not elected on either occasion. He was sent to Barming Asylum, but released into the care of a religious fanatic,

George Francis, Boughton-under-Blean, 1837 (See Boughton-under-Blean—Francis). He set himself up as a Messiah at a time of rural unrest among farm labourers, playing on their humble status and religious beliefs, and gathered a band of followers. When numbers began to decline he started open disorder. A constable, John Mears, with two other men (See Boughton-under-Blean—Mears) was sent to arrest Tom who shot Nicholas Mears. The army was summoned from Canterbury and Tom and his followers were trapped in Bossenden Wood near Dunkirk on 31st May 1838. Lieutenant Bennett (see Canterbury—Bennett) was shot by Tom at point blank range. The soldiers fired and Tom with seven of his followers fell dead, seven more being wounded and some dying later. A special constable from Faversham named Catt was also killed accidentally in the crossfire. Some of Tom's followers went to prison, others were released, three were transported. Tom's dead followers and the others killed were interred either at Hernhill or Boughton-under-Blean. The seven at Boughton were Stephen Baker, William Foster, William Rye, Edward Wraight, Phineas Harvey, William Burford and George Branchett. Tom was interred in an unmarked grave slightly to the left of the path and about twenty feet from the north wall of the nave, with very little religious ceremony, in St Michael's Churchyard, Hernhill. At first it was intended that the other dead followers were to be interred alongside Tom in a row of nameless graves, but this plan was changed so that they were interred in various parts of Hernhill Churchyard near their relatives. For several days the place where Tom was interred was guarded in case any of his followers decided to dig down to see if Tom had been resurrected as he said he would be. No-one did. Today there is no trace of the grave.

HEVER

Boleyn, Sir Thomas (Sir Thomas Bullen) (d. 1538). Knight of the Garter. Father of Anne Boleyn, second wife of Henry VIII; grandfather of Elizabeth I. Brass and tomb in the Boleyn Chapel, St Peter's Church, Hever.

HIGH HALDEN

In the churchyard of St Mary's Church, High Halden, is an oak 'pyramid', about five feet high, without inscription. It does not mark the site of a grave, but is reputed to be a memorial to an unknown suicide. As was customary the body is believed to have been interred either on the north side of the church or locally in unconsecrated ground. (Sometimes suicides were buried at crossroads or three-went ways). (See Harbledown—Anderson; Ickham-de Baa). In this instance the deceased's friends were allowed to erect this plain wood structure in the churchyard. Igglesden refers to it existing around the turn of the century.

HOATH

Steed, Richard (1808-1863). Murder Victim. Violently killed during a quarrel on a footpath near Maypole, concerning a debt of money, on 3rd May 1863, by Alfred Eldridge, a railway navvy. Eldridge, aged 32, was found guilty at his trial at Maidstone Assizes (he later confessed to the crime), sentenced to death and publicly hanged on 20th August 1863, on a scaffold outside Maidstone Prison. Steed was interred in the Church of the Holy Cross Churchyard, Hoath. (See Hoo St Werburgh—White; Ightham—Luard; Southborough—O'Rourke; Throwley—Sondes).

HOLLINGBOURNE

Colepeper, Lady Elizabeth (1582-1638). The mother of the four daughters: Elizabeth (interred in the same church, 1709); Judith (interred same church, 1691); Philippa and another Philippa, who made the famous Colepeper altar cloth, 1650-60. On her tomb is a life-sized recumbent effigy of Elizabeth in white marble, the sculptor being Edward Marshal. What is notable is that on each hand she is wearing a ring, both rings being attached to the wrist by a fine cord. This fashion began in the 17th century and is said to have started when James I gave one of his rings to a lady at court, but as the ring was too large in order not to lose it she tied it to her wrist and other ladies copied her. Interred in All Saints' Church, Hollingbourne.

Gethin, Dame Grace (1676-1697). Died, aged 21, probably of a broken heart. According to the diary of her aunt, Elizabeth Freke: '1697. February 16th, my deer Neece and God-daughter and my deer sister Norton's only child, was privately married to Sr Richard Gettings, an Irish baronet, who soon brok her Hartt; and on the 11th October following she gave upp her pious soule to God. She lyes buryed amongst all our relations, wher there lyes neer three score of them in Hollingburne Chancell'. Interred in the chancel of All Saints' Church, Hollingbourne, where there is also a memorial. In 1842 during work in the chancel her skeleton and remains were witnessed inside the altar rails, the skeleton being described as that of a very small person.

Hasted, Edward (1760-1855). Son of Edward Hasted, author of the famous 'History of Kent'. Vicar of Hollingbourne for 70 years, 1785-1855. Died unmarried. Believed interred in the chancel of All Saints' Church, Hollingbourne, where there is a memorial. In 1842 a Miss Hasted *was* interred in the chancel, but the relationship is unknown.

Reynolds (Rainoles), William (d.1543). An inscription on an altar tomb near the porch is probably the oldest legible memorial in a Kent churchyard: 'Here Lieth William Rainoles and Jon his Wife. He was buried the 4 of July 1543'. All Saints' Churchyard, Hollingbourne. (See Cranbrook—Courthope; Stockbury—Gover)

HOO ST. WERBURGH

Aveling, Thomas (1824-1882). Founder of Steam Road Traction. A farmer at Ruckinge until he started making agricultural implements at Rochester, he was an engine builder there from 1860 until his death. He was the first to build a traction engine with a single cylinder and also invented steam road rollers. He was a partner in the company that made traction engines, Aveling & Porter. On 7th March 1982, the centenary of his death, the Road Roller Association held a meeting in Rochester and then drove in a procession of ten steam engines from Boley Hill House, his old home in Rochester, to Hoo St Werburgh Churchyard and a wreath was then laid on his grave during a short service at the graveside. Interred on the north-east side of Hoo St Werburgh Churchyard.

White, William (d.1808). Murder Victim. According to the very long inscription on his gravestone, some of which is now defective and goes into the earth, White 'yeoman, who was on the Sunday evening 11th December 1808, most barbarously murdered in the bosom of his afflicted family, by a gun discharged at him through a window, whilst sitting by his fireside . . . He left issue of 6 sons and 5 daughters. 'By whose assassinating hand I fell, Rests yet conceal'd and none but God can tell'.' The murderer was never discovered but was thought to be one of his own sons, though nothing was ever proved against him and he later died in New South Wales where he had been transported for another felony. Interred, with his wife, on the north-east side of Hoo St Werburgh Churchyard. (See Hoath—Steed; Ightham—Luard; Newington-next-Sittingbourne—Bouser; Southborough—O'Rourke; Throwley—Sondes).

HORSMONDEN

Smith-Marriott, Rev. Sir William Marriott (1807-1864). The most notable member of a local family that provided Horsmonden with squires and rectors for some 159 years, who was himself incumbent for nearly 40 years. A lover of Sir Walter Scott's literary works, he had built a tower, known later as 'Scott's Tower', on high ground about a quarter to half a mile from the Smith-Marriott rectory. Although so-named it comprised two towers, both battlemented, one higher than the other and with a room that formed a museum and library of Scott's works. The 'Tower' became unsafe and in the 1950s was demolished. Interred in the family vault in St Margaret's Churchyard, Horsmonden. This church also contains a memorial bust in the south aisle to **John Read** (d.1847), who was employed as agent on the Smith-Marriott estate and placed therein on his decease by the family. He was also an inventor, in 1823 inventing a stomach pump and in 1840 a 'drowned man resuscitator'. It is uncertain but probable that he was also interred in Horsmonden Churchyard.

Within sight of the sea the lifeboat pioneer Lionel Lukin's headstone in St Leonard's Churchyard, Hythe.
(Photograph by the author)

The crypt, St Leonard's Church, Hythe, with its collection of bones and skulls.
(Published by J. Davis, Queen Victoria Street, London, c.1902, postcard in author's collection)

HOTHFIELD

Stanford, Sarah (d.1790). Smallpox Victim. Her headstone bears the epitaph: 'Her soul without a spot is gone to Heaven; Her spotted body to the worms is given'. Interred by a yew tree that stands alongside the path through the churchyard that leads to the west door of St Mary's Church, Hothfield. Other smallpox victims are Goudhurst—Freeman; Ightham—Lambarde; Pluckley—Nepecker; Sundridge—Clavell.

HUNTON

Borton, Arthur Drummond (1883-1933). Victoria Cross Winner. Lt-Col, C.M.G., D.S.O. Served in the army in South Africa, but was sent home as unfit for service in 1908. On outbreak of First World War he joined the Royal Flying Corps as an observer, but broke his neck in an aircraft crash and for the second time was invalided home as unfit for service in 1914. Rejoined the army and was at the Dardanelles landing, then served in France and Salonika. He won his V.C. at Lel-el-Sheria, Palestine, November 1917, becoming famous for the attack against the Turks in which he and his men, ten volunteers, dribbled a football as they went forward and secured a Turkish field battery. Interred in the extension to St Mary the Virgin's Churchyard, Hunton, about midway along the hedge bordering the road.

Fane, Sir Thomas (d.1606). Lieutenant of Dover Castle. **Dame Helen Somersett** (d.1606) was his wife for 40 years. Interred in St Mary the Virgin's Church, Hunton. He is noteworthy because of his alabaster monument in the Sanctuary, which not only shows him reclining lifesized with his wife but also bears the figures of their daughter Mary who died in 'childbed' (see Hartlip—Coppin; Stockbury—Ruffin) and her son Thomas who died shortly afterwards. Sir Thomas Fane was related to the Fane family, Tudeley, of whom there were several named Sir Thomas Fane. There is a monument to his grandfather in Tudeley Church.

HYTHE

Lukin, Lionel (1742-1834). London Coachmaker. Inventor of the First Practical, Successful Lifeboat. Part of the lengthy inscription reads: 'This Lionel Lukin was the first who built a Life Boat and was the original inventor of that Principle of Safety by which many lives and much property have been preserved from shipwreck and he obtained for it the King's Patent in the year 1785'. Interred near the west door of St Leonard's Church, Hythe, near a churchyard path and lamp-post. The headstone has recently been cleaned and restored.

Pettit-Smith, Sir Francis (1808-1874). Inventor of Screw Propulsion. Began as a local farmer on Romney Marsh, but was interested in and experimented with ship propulsion. In 1835 he constructed a model propelled by a screw activated by a spring. In 1836 he took out a patent and built a boat fitted with it, which was tested at Ramsgate, Dover and Hythe. It was used as a means of propulsion for the 237 ton S.S. *Archimedes* on trial on the Thames and at Sheerness, then tested against S.S. *Vulcan*, a fast paddle-steamer, 1839, and proved successful. The Royal Navy was now convinced and gave an order for its use in H.M.S. *Rattler*, the first screw steamer in the Royal Navy, built at Sheerness. Brunel had already been impressed and he changed the design for his *Great Britain* from a paddle steamer to a vessel fitted with screw propulsion. Pettit-Smith's birthplace over a shop in Hythe High Street is known as 'Propeller House'. Twice married, first to Ann Buck of Folkestone, 1830, by whom he had two sons, then to Susannah Wallis of Boxley. His two sons and second wife outlived him. Interred in St Leonard's Churchyard, Hythe, several rows west of Lionel Lukin's grave, there being a gravestone, the legible part reading 'Archimedes Pettit-Smith aged 7'.

Skull and Bones Collection. At St Leonard's Church, Hythe, there is an ossuary or charnel house containing the remains of some 4,000 people, former inhabitants of Hythe. Various suggestions have been made as to the origin of the bones, one being that they are the remains of plague victims, and another that they were the dead of a battle fought in the vicinity. Several experts have examined the bones in the past and found them to be in fact bones of medieval people who lived in the Hythe area, possibly up to the late 15th century. They would originally have been interred in the churchyard and then after a period of time, and when the site was needed for another corpse, the bones would be dug up and placed in the ossuary known as the 'crypt'. There are several hundred skulls on shelves and stacks of various other bones. Among them is a skull that has been trepanned to relieve pressure on the brain: the skull owner lived after the operation! Some skulls have good teeth while those of others are worn down by the coarse food. There is also a very large skull of a man who must have been a giant. Hair that also survived burial is preserved and on display. The collection is open at certain times on payment of admission, a long-established custom. In 1816 a Richard Chamberlain was 'allowed the sum of £1 in addition to his present salary of £4 a year and the privilege of shewing the bones.'

ICKHAM

de Baa, Sir Thomas (d.1339). Interred in the south transept, the Baye Transept, St John's Church, Ickham, his tomb having an effigy of him on it in full armour. According to Igglesden 'The south transept is called the Baa Chapel because it belonged to a family of that name who owned Baa Farm'. On the ancient foundations of the latter was built Baye House and Farm in Baye Lane, perhaps a later version of the earlier name? The area formed by the junction of Baye Lane with lanes to Seaton and to Britton Farm was a burial site for suicides. (See High Halden)

Heghtresbury, William (Will proved 1372). Professor of the Sacred Page (learned in Holy Scripture). Chancellor of Oxford University. Rector of

Ickham, instituted 1354. Interred in St John's Church, Ickham. In a recess in the north wall of the north transept there is a reclining effigy of the Rector wearing a cap, his feet on a dog.

Pettman, Robert (1615-1685). Brewer. According to Mee he gave money in 1670 to ransom Englishmen captured by the Turks. Perhaps his generosity earned him his interment beneath a floor slab, alongside an admiral, near the chancel altar rails in St John's Church, Ickham.

Swann, Frederick Dashwood (1796-1870). Captain, Grenadier Guards. Fought in the Peninsular Campaign and the Battle of Waterloo. Interred on the righthand side near the porch of the south door, St John's Church, Ickham.

IGHTHAM

Cawne, Sir Thomas (d.1374?). First known owner of Ightham Mote, he probably built the Great Hall. His tomb with life-sized effigy is contemporary with the famous one of Edward, the Black Prince, in Canterbury Cathedral. He is dressed in a mixture of plate and mail, as worn at the Battle of Crecy, and it is particularly finely carved. Interred in St Peter's Church, Ightham.

Farebrace (Firebrass), Henry (d.1601?). Founder of the surviving Firebrass Charity. Rector of Ightham 1574-1586, he resigned to become Vicar of Farningham 1589-1601, where he died. He bequeathed to the poor of Ightham 20 shillings per annum obtained from the rent of a field, 'Bearfield' off Oldbury Lane, Ightham, now a house site, 'Heronshaw'. He made a similar benefaction for the poor of Farningham. Both are recorded on his brass in St Peter & St Paul's Church, Farningham, where he was interred. In his book 'Ightham—Notes on Local History' 1978, Edward Bowra gives the name of the founder of this Charity as the variant Firebrass.

Harrison, Benjamin (1837-1921). Grocer. Archaeologist. Discovered flints in the Pre-Glacial Drift on the North Downs that were artefacts, (he called them eoliths), used by prehistoric man. One of the first examples he found, in 1865, is mounted above a memorial tablet to him in St Peter's Church, Ightham, where he was interred in the churchyard north-west of the church tower. His epitaph is quoted from Shakespeare's 'As You Like It': 'He found in life "Books in the running brooks, sermons in stones and good in everything".'

James, Richard (1746-1807). A Receiver-General for Kent. J.P. Colonel of the West Kent Militia. After 29 years military service, including being at Portsmouth when the Fleet mutinied at Spithead, he was appointed Receiver-General, 1792, with responsibility for raising all taxes and duties for 'His Majesty's Exchequer', covering about a third of the Kent population. The revenue collection varied from land and property taxes to duty on horse dealers, lights, windows, male servants, carriages, horses, dogs, clocks, watches, armorial bearings, even hair powder! Last of the notable James family of Ightham to hold the right of patronage of the church. Interred with many of his ancestors in the family vault beneath the Manor pews in St Peter's Church, Ightham.

Kemble, Adelaide (1816-1879). Opera Singer of distinction, notably in the part of Norma, but retired on marriage in 1843 to Edward Sartoris, M.P. for Carmarthenshire 1868-1874. Author of 'A Week in a French Country House', 1867, 'Medusa and Other Tales', 1868, 'Past Hours', published posthumously 1880. Youngest daughter of Charles Kemble (1775-1854) actor; younger sister of Fanny Kemble (1809-1893), writer and actress. Her aunt was Sarah Siddons, the tragic actress. Their connection with Ightham was that their daughter, May, married Henry Evans-Gordon of Prestons Farm House, Ightham. May died in 1925 and is interred near Adelaide Kemble and her husband, Edward Sartoris (1817-1888) to the north-west of the tower in St Peter's Churchyard, Ightham.

Lambarde, Jane (1553-1573). First wife of William Lambarde (1536-1601), author of 'A Perambulation of Kent', 1576 (interred in Greenwich, then Sevenoaks Church). Daughter of George Multon, St Clere, Ightham, she married Lambarde in 1570. Died of smallpox (see Hothfield—Stanford), aged 21 and was interred in St Peter's Church, Ightham. Her tombstone is situated in the wall by the vestry door, on which in relief is an arch ornamented with a moulding of Gothic leaves and columns and the remains of a brass. The damaged condition of the stone is due to it having been moved at least twice from its original position. The brass was stolen in the 19th century and only fragments recovered.

Luard, Caroline (d.1908). Murder Victim. On 24th August 1908, she took her dogs for a walk from her home at Ightham Knoll to some woods nearby. When she had not returned by tea-time her husband Major-General Luard searched for her and found her dead body in woodland with bullet wounds in her head. The police found no clues to her murderer nor motive for the murder. Local gossip, accompanied by vicious poison-pen letters, threw suspicion on her husband although he was a benefactor of the church and village and a churchwarden for 20 years. The strain became too much and three weeks after her death he committed suicide by throwing himself in front of a train. Interred near Adelaide Kemble's grave to the north-west of the tower of St Peter's Church, Ightham. (See Hoath—Steed; Hoo St Werburgh—White; Southborough—O'Rourke; Throwley—Sondes)

Selby, Dame Dorothy (1572-1641). She has been credited with being one of those who exposed the Gunpowder Plot. A cultured person, fine needlewoman and embroiderer. The epitaph on her monument states 'She was a Dorcas, Whose curious needle turned the abused stage Of this lewd world into the golden age; Prudently simple, providently wary. To the world a Martha and to Heaven a Mary.' She worked the pictures 'Golden Age', 'Acts of Jonah' and 'Gunpowder Plot'. The epitaph continues 'Whose art disclos'd that plot which had it taken, Rome had tryumphed and Britain's walls had shaken . . .'. A panel of her monument shows her version of the Armada and the Gunpowder Plot, the original needlework still surviving. It is unlikely that she was involved in the Plot's discovery but too much emphasis was placed on her epitaph wording 'Whose art disclos'd the Plot' which meant no more than that she depicted it as one of her needlework pictures. Dorothy Selby's interment is not recorded in the church burial register but this is not of any significance and as there is a Selby vault in the church containing ten coffins it is likely she was interred in the vault or within the church of St Peter's, Ightham.

Sutton, William (1830-1888). Victoria Cross Winner. In 1857 while serving as a bugler, 6th Rifles, he won his V.C. for outstanding valour at the siege of Delhi. In St Catherine's Chapel, Ightham Church, is a brass commemorative plaque placed there in 1972 by his regiment, now the Royal Green Jackets, who possess his V.C. in their museum, Winchester. He was interred in St Peter's Churchyard, Ightham, although the grave site is apparently now unknown.

KENNINGTON

Culver, Sarah (1793-1875). One of the women followers of John Tom (Sir William Courtenay) (see Hernhill). She lived with her mother and father at Bossenden Farm at the time of the 'rebellion' in 1838. After Tom was killed in Blean Woods she washed and laid out his body still fanatically believing he was asleep and would arise again on the third day. After his funeral she returned to live at the farm with her parents but eventually left and lived at The Lawn, Kennington, where she died a spinster, still firmly believing in Tom's cause. (See Boughton-under-Blean—Francis) Interred in St Mary's Churchyard, Kennington.

Jones, John (born 23rd December 1798—died 23rd December 1862). For 45 years Servant in the family of H.W. Carter, of Kennington Hall. Interred in St Mary's Churchyard, Kennington. (See Ashford—Waters; Eastwell—Hill; Godmersham—Sackree)

Parker, Ann (1729-1837). Centenarian. Known as 'Granny Parker'. Died in her 108th year leaving one daughter, Elizabeth, aged 81. Interred on the east side of the south entrance of St Mary's Churchyard, Kennington, the headstone being 'erected by voluntary contributions.' (See Boughton-under-Blean—Hawkins; Maidstone—Fancett)

KESTON

Bealknap (or Belknap), Sir Robert de (d.1400). Judge. Lord of the Manor of Hempstead, near Chatham, 14th century. He granted lands near Chatham to the Prior and Convent of Rochester. In 1365 and 1369 he was one of the

The grave of Mrs Craik in Keston Churchyard. (Photograph by courtesy of Kenneth Miller, Beckenham)

Commissioners appointed to survey the Thanet coast and take measures to secure the properties and land in the area against sea erosion and in 1372 was a member of a Commission entrusted with the defence of Kent against invasion. In 1381 he was involved with Wat Tyler's rebellion and was compelled by the rebels not to sit in judgment on them. He agreed not to enforce the law in order to escape with his life. He was later charged with treason and sentenced to death but this was commuted to banishment to Ireland and his lands were confiscated. In 1397 he was recalled to England and restored to his rights and lands. Interred near the steps to the chancel of Keston Church (no dedication).

Craik, Mrs. (Dinah Maria Mulock) (1826-1887). Novelist. Her best known work is 'John Halifax, Gentleman', 1857. She also wrote children's stories and poetry. In 1864/5? married George L. Craik, a partner in the publishing company, Macmillan. She lived at The Corner House, Shortlands, from 1865 until her death. Interred in Keston Churchyard, Keston (no church dedication) near a hedge border under a Celtic Cross.

KNOWLTON

Narbrough, Sir John (1640-1688). Admiral. Fought against the Tripoli Corsairs, 1674, and Algerian Corsairs, 1677. He went to Barbados, successfully recovering treasure from wrecks, ('treasure fishing'), but eventually caught a fever and died May 1688. It was planned to embalm the body but it was found impossible and so he was buried at sea the following day, but before that the 'bowels' were removed and preserved to be brought back to England. These were interred in St. Clement's Church, Knowlton, where he had an estate, although the memorial to him states: 'Here lie the remains of Sir John Narbrough.' Narbrough married twice. His second wife was Elizabeth (d.1732, See Shovell, Crayford) who survived him and married Sir Cloudisley Shovell. Her two sons by Narbrough, John and James, were serving with their stepfather Shovell when their ship H.M.S. *Association* was wrecked on the Scilly Isles, and both were drowned. Their memorial in the same church has a bas-relief of the doomed ship and the inscription 'Happy in their Inclinations, Happy in their Fortunes, Unhappy only in their Fate.' Narbrough's daughter, Elizabeth, (b.1682) married Sir Thomas D'Aeth, 1701, but died 1721 and is also interred in the chancel of Knowlton Church.

LEEDS

Barham, James (1725-1818). Bellringer for 60 years, 'from the year 1744 to the year 1804 in Kent and elsewhere'. Some of his bellringing feats are listed on his headstone in St Nicholas Churchyard, Leeds.

LENHAM

Honywood, Mary, née Waters (1527-1620). Celebrated for her longevity and the large number of lineal descendants she lived to see. Born at Lenham, in 1543 when 16 she married Robert Honywood of Charing and Marks Hall, Essex, by whom she had 16 children. 'At her decease she had 367 children lawfully descended from her, 16 of her own body, 114 grandchildren, 228 great-grandchildren and 9 great-great-grandchildren'—details from a brass by the altar in the church, this brass being in memory of her grandchild Robert Thompson. One of her grandchildren, Dr. Michael Honywood (1597-1681), Dean of Lincoln, used to tell of his having been present at a banquet given to her by her descendants, 200 of whom sat down with her to table. She is mentioned in Foxe's 'Book of Martyrs' for her prison work. Also noted for her piety but in old age she became despondent. It is recorded by John Foxe on a visit to console her that in front of him she 'dashed a Venice glass to the ground saying 'Sir, I am as sure to be damned as this glass is to be broke' when by God's wonderful providence the glass was taken up uninjured'. She died at Marks Hall, May 1620, and, according to the Dictionary of National Biography, was interred at Lenham on 20th May, probably in St Mary's Church, but the site is not indicated.

LEYBOURNE

Heart Shrines. In a low recess in a wall, under a canopy, are two stone caskets. The one on the left carved with a cinquefoil contains a small lead casket in which is the heart of Sir Roger Leybourne who died in 1271 while en route to the Holy Land on a Crusade. The stone casket on the right carved with two arches, intended for his wife, is empty because she re-married. In St Peter & St Paul's Church, Leybourne.

In the shade of sycamore trees the table tomb of 'sportsman' Henry Denne, Littlebourne Churchyard. In the left background is the monument on the grave of Adela Wyman. (Photograph by the author)

LINTON

Mann, Sir Horace (1701-1786). Spy and Envoy. In 1737 he was appointed by Sir Robert Walpole to the post of Associate to 'Mr. Fane', Envoy Extraordinary and Minister Plenipotentiary at the Court of Florence. In 1746 he succeeded 'Fane', his main task being to watch the activities of the Old Pretender to the English throne and his family in Italy, relating mostly gossip that damaged the reputation of the last of the Stuarts. For his spying activities he is known to have used ciphers. In 1755 he succeeded to the family estate at Linton. For 44 years he corresponded with Horace Walpole from Italy, his letters giving us an insight to Italian life and customs of that time. He died in Florence, 1786, after 46 years as British Envoy there. His body was returned to England and interred in St Nicholas Church, Linton.

LITTLEBOURNE

Denne, Henry (1755-1822). Sportsman! Landowner, the Dennes having been Lords of the Manor of Littlebourne for several generations, living at Elbridge. Between 1770 and 1809 he shot 2,322 partridges, 753 pheasants, 2,079 hares, 3,764 rabbits, 1,682 woodcock, 2,552 snipe, 600 wildfowl, 700 landrail and two eagles. Death eventually shot him down on 6th August 1822. In his last wishes he requested a perched black eagle to be carved in a cartouche at each end of his table tomb: 'The game I killed in my sporting days from the first day I carried a gun till the last. On the head the first eagle I shot in 1770 and on the foot the second eagle shot in 1797. On one side all the feathered tribe in detail each sort and on the other side the fur and flesh animals'. Permission to do this was not given even though Denne had been a churchwarden. He was only allowed to have the two eagles on his tomb as he had instructed. Interred with his two wives (first, Sarah Hollingbury, aged 17, d.1809, and, second, Elizabeth Whittle, aged 79, d.1836), in a recently restored tomb under sycamore trees on the north side of St Vincent's Churchyard, Littlebourne. He also left instructions in his Will that his second wife on her death was to be interred in the same tomb with himself and his first wife and the tomb was to be enlarged to hold all three so they would be all together, as they are.

Wyman, Adela (1848-1864). Daughter of an Inca Princess. Alongside the Henry Denne table tomb on the north side of St Vincent's Churchyard, Littlebourne, under sycamore trees, is a grave to various members of the Wyman family. Of these John Wyman, schoolmaster, had several sons who travelled the world, one to China, two others to Peru. One of the latter sons married an Inca Princess. The daughter of this union, Adela, visited England in 1862. Eventually taken ill, probably with consumption, she died in 1864 aged 16. The stone was erected over her grave in memory of her and of John and Frances Wyman by two surviving sons, William and Henry Wyman.

LYDD

Austin, Annie Antivaccinator (1892-1967). What's in a name? One cannot help wondering what the vicar thought when the parents presented their daughter for baptism and told him the intended Christian names, unless this was a name she took herself through holding strong convictions concerning vaccination. Interred in the new cemetery, Lydd. (See Hothfield—Stanford; Pluckley—Nepecker; Sundridge—Mompesson)

Edgar, Thomas (1745-1801). Lieut., R.N. First Mate on the *Resolution* with Captain Cook on his circumnavigation of the world, 1776-80, he was present when Cook was murdered, 1779. He gave evidence at the enquiry into the circumstances of Cook's death. The inscription states that Cook was killed 'by the Indians at Owhie in the South Seas'. This spelling was probably a local Romney Marsh stonemason's way of saying Hawaii. The epitaph also states the date was 14th February 1778, but this is incorrect and should be 1779. The inscription for Edgar reads: 'Tom Edgar at last has sailed out of this world, His shroud is put on, His topsails are furled, He lies snug in death's boat without any concern And is moored for a full due ahead and astern. O'er the Compass of Life he had merrily run, His voyage is completed, his reckoning is done'. Interred in All Saints' Churchyard, Lydd. In the 1950s an anonymous donor paid for this gravestone and that of Sisley to be restored and the lettering recut.

Greenland, Edward (1853-1870). Empty Grave of Drowned Man. He fell from the rigging of H.M.S. *Barossa* off Yokohama and was drowned 28th February 1870, aged 17. The stone in the churchyard of All Saints' Church, Lydd, records: 'This stone is erected by Lieutenant C.E. Drake of H.M.S. *Barossa* as a mark of esteem and regret felt by himself and the crew'. But was Greenland's body brought all the way home from Japan preserved for burial, or is the cross and tombstone a memorial only, with no grave below? It seems the latter is the case. There is no entry in the Lydd register to Edward Greenland being interred there at that time or later. The Greenland family was an old established one in Lydd, there being records of them living there from 1686. It was appropriate therefore that a memorial cross and tombstone to Edward, born in Lydd, baptised there 9th January 1853, should be erected in the churchyard.

Lepper, Henry (1788-1883). Town Sergeant of Lydd for 65 years. Interred in All Saints' Churchyard, Lydd.

Sisley, Francis (1748-1808). Farmer and Grazier. Smuggler. Known for his daring exploits. He was involved in the 'guinea trade' during the Napoleonic Wars, but specialised in silks. He sent his eldest son Thomas to Dunkirk, France, where he built up a highly successful 'branch' to his father's 'free trade' smuggling organisation. Thomas stayed in France, married, and became a respectable trader in silks and Paisley shawls. Alfred Sisley (1839-1899), the French Impressionist painter, was descended from Francis Sisley. The latter's daughter Elizabeth married a William Sell, a Lydd saddler and smuggler, who was arrested, convicted and imprisoned in Dover Castle. On release he obtained a job in the prison and was eventually appointed 'Boder', Keeper of the Debtors' Prison, in Dover Castle! Francis is interred in All Saints' Churchyard, Lydd. In the 1950s an anonymous donor paid for this and the gravestone of Edgar to be restored and the lettering recut.

Strugell, Thomas and **John**. In Lydd Churchyard is a monument that is claimed to have read: 'Heare lyeth Thomas Strugell and John Strugell, His Sonne, who have boath hed baliefes and iurats of this Towne of Lydd many years. Thomas dyed February Anno 1551. John dyed December Anno 1581'. If accurate this is probably one of the, if not the oldest memorials in a Kent churchyard. (See Cranbrook, Hollingbourne, Stockbury)

Stuppeny, Clement (1525-1608). Jurat of Lydd, 1565, later Bailiff, around whose tomb the Commonalty assembled to elect the Jurats of Lydd. Great-grandson of Richard Stuppenye of New Romney (see New Romney —Stuppenye) around whose tomb in that church the Jurats assembled to elect their Mayor. In the North Chapel, All Saints' Church, Lydd.

Walker, George (1783-1819). Smuggler. Killed by a sword thrust inflicted by a Blockade Man, Lieut. Peatt, on 1st August 1819. Another version says

80

Walker was shot. His illegible epitaph forgives his killer: 'Let it be known that I am clay, A base man took my life away, Yet freely do I him forgive, And hope in Heaven we both shall live. Wife and children I've left behind, and to the Lord I them resign, I hope He will their steps attend And guide them to a happy end'. Interred in All Saints' Churchyard, Lydd

Waylett, William (1728-1815). Man-Midwife and Doctor, Lydd area. In the 18th century it was usual for midwives to be male to attend birth officially, but no doubt unofficially some unqualified local woman performed the task at times for very poor women at lower cost. The man-midwife had a scale of fees charged according to circumstances and distances involved, varying from the half-guinea Poor Law Fee to four guineas. Interred without a memorial stone in the chancel of All Saints' Church, Lydd.

Sea Disaster Victims. In All Saints' Churchyard, Lydd, is a headstone 'Sacred to the Memory of Henry Huddart (Master), Alfred Barnes, Charles Chisent, George Ross, Jean Esquare, Charles Mariner, William Mason, William Liverpool, Charles Mason, Jean Francois, William Davis and John Deane, of the barque *Enchantress* of Whitehaven wrecked near Lydd Station, 26th October 1855'. The entire crew numbered thirteen, one of whom, the First Mate, was saved. In the grave are interred the Master and seven of his crew.

LYMPNE

Bachelour, Captain Isaac (1644-1681 or 4). Army Officer, with an interesting and rather humorous inscription now worn smooth by the feet of past generations of Lympne schoolchildren attending school, the marble floor slab being in the north aisle, against the south wall. It reads: 'Here lieth interred the body of Captain Isaac Bachelour who being commissioned to serve His Majesty under the honourable title in the Militia for the County was discharged by death the 26th May 1684(1?) aged 40; whose sorrowful widow, Mrs Mary Bachelour, as a pledge of respect to his surviving memory, placed this stone for an imperfect monument of his desert and her affection'. This verse followed:

> 'Since a life-vanquished Captain here doth lie
> Death hath a sting and grave a victory,
> But hold! Can he be vanquished whose last breath
> Challenged the grave and triumphed over death?
> No, but he changed his quarters and marched on
> To meet the Captain of his salvation
> Under whose more auspicious command
> He is now commissioned in a better land,
> Where soldiers are all Saints — Heaven is the prize
> And prayers and praises the sole exercise.
> Thus fights our Captain and proclaims his cause
> In thundering peals of Halleluias'.

Interred in St Stephen's Church, Lympne.

Damer-Dawson, Margaret (1875-1920). Founder of the Women Police Service, 1915, after being Co-founder, with Nina Boyle, of the Women Police Volunteers, 1914. She created a small group of 'motoring ladies' whose job was to meet refugee trains arriving from Belgium. She was also Agent to the Minister of Munitions for the training, supplying and controlling of a force of policewomen in H.M. Munition Factories, 1915. As early as 1908 the Home Office had instituted 'police matrons' and from these, with private security organisations, a sort of women police developed, culminating in the Women Police Service, of which Margaret Damer-Dawson was appointed Chief Officer. Official aid and support was given when it was seen what a useful job these women did, particularly in clearing the streets of drunks. The Service even included militant suffragettes, some of whom had police records! In 1918 when Metropolitan Police Women Patrols were formed those already in the Women Police Service, however, were rejected for the new force, possibly due to the miscellaneous characters who had made up the W.P.S.! She was awarded the O.B.E. in 1918 for her work with women police. In early life she had worked for the protection of animals in England and in Europe, 1903-1914, being awarded a silver medal by the King of Denmark for this work. Interred in St Stephen's Churchyard, Lympne. (See Brenchley—Ruxton)

Finch, John (d.1707). In his Will he left land at Lympne, Eastbridge and Newchurch, a portion of the rent to be given to a number of poor people of Lympne, one half of the sum on the date of his burial, 7th February, the other half on the Sunday after Christmas Day, an example of one of the few Christmas charities in Kent. Interred beneath a floor slab in the chancel, within the altar rails, in St Stephen's Church, Lympne. (See Dymchurch— Bedingfield)

LYNSTED

Dacre, Lady Ann (burial date 23rd May 1722). Illegitimate daughter of Charles II and Lady Castlemaine, who married the 8th Baron Teynham and is interred in the mausoleum adjoining the Roper Chapel, St Peter & St Paul's Church, Lynsted.

Hugessen, James (d.1646). 'Merchant Adventurer' (in modern parlance a trader, probably one who sailed abroad and brought back goods to sell here and took goods with him to sell at places of call, a sort of importer-exporter). The Hugessens intermarried with the Knatchbull family. Although he came from Dover he is interred near the chancel, St Peter & St Paul's Church, Lynsted, as he had purchased Sewards (known now as Lynsted Court) in Charles I's reign.

Roper, Christopher (d.1558/9). Escheator (Confiscator of Property for the King) for Kent, 1550. Youngest son of John Roper, Sheriff of Kent, 1521 (d.1524 and interred in Roper Vault, St Dunstan's Church, Canterbury). Brother of William Roper (d.1578, biographer of Sir Thomas More and also interred in the same Roper Vault, Canterbury (see also Canterbury)). Grandfather of Sir John Roper, 1st Baron Teynham (see below). Interred in the Roper Chapel, St Peter & Paul's Church, Lynsted. (See Farningham—Roper)

Roper, Christopher (d.1624). 2nd Baron Teynham. His magnificent tomb is notable for having two panels of sculpture by Epiphanius Evesham, the first great English sculptor, whose work is uncommon in Kent churches. Roper's effigy is lying on his back with his feet on a lion and a red cloak over his armour. Behind him is a life-like effigy of his kneeling wife, her hands clasped in prayer and her long brown hair seemingly blown back by the wind. Interred in the Roper Chapel, St Peter & St Paul's Church, Lynsted. (See Farningham—Roper)

Roper, Sir John (d.1618). 1st Baron Teynham. Custos Brevium (Keeper of the County Law Records and Archives, also in office at the Court of the King's Bench). According to Hasted he was made 1st Baron Teynham in 1616 by James I because Roper had been the first notable person to proclaim James was king in the county of Kent, but in fact Roper bought his barony, paying £10,000 for it, this money going to the Exchequer. Roper was 82 and lived only another two years to enjoy the title. Interred in an impressive marble tomb with his effigy in the Roper Chapel, St Peter & St Paul's Church, Lynsted.

MAIDSTONE

Astley, Sir Jacob (1579-1652/3). Royalist Soldier. Fought in various European armies and then in that of Charles I after the outbreak of the Civil War, 1642. Fought at the Battle of Edgehill and was one of those 'hurt'. Prior to the start he composed the famous prayer: 'O Lord, Thou knowest how busy I must be this day. If I forget Thee, do not Thou forget me'. As a Royalist he was imprisoned in the Fleet but was released on bail and died in the Old Palace, Maidstone. Interred in All Saints' Church, Maidstone. On a wall below the west window is a memorial to him that is also believed to be his tomb.

Astley, John (d.1595). Master of the Queen's Jewel House, appointed by Elizabeth I 1558. Treasurer of Her Majesty's Jewels and Plate. Master of the Game, Enfield Chase and Park. In 1568 he leased the Manor and Castle of Allington. Author of 'The Art of Riding'. His son,by his second wife, also Sir John Astley, was Master of the Revels to James I and Charles I. Both, with their wives, are interred in All Saints' Church, Maidstone. At the west end of the Church are four figures and a table monument, all part of one memorial to them.

Courtenay, William (d.1396). Archbishop of Canterbury. Obtained a Licence from Richard II to found a Collegiate Church, staffed by a college of priests, at Maidstone in 1395. Much of the building work survives as All

Saints, though the college was suppressed in 1547. He asked in his last wishes to be interred in this church he founded at Maidstone. Originally what is reputed to be his tomb with a brass indent stood three feet above floor level in the centre of the chancel but this was eventually lowered to floor level as can now be seen. There is, however, a tomb for Archbishop Courtenay on the south side of the Trinity Chapel, Canterbury Cathedral. When Courtenay died Richard II was at Canterbury and presumably Courtenay was with him. Richard then probably ordered the archbishop to be buried in the cathedral and a tomb supposedly containing his body is near that of the Black Prince in the Trinity Chapel. The information board at Maidstone church also states that Courtenay was interred at Canterbury. However, in 1794 the Courtenay tomb at Maidstone was opened to reveal a skeleton, but there was no ring or any item contained inside to confirm there had been interment of an archbishop. This implies that against his wish he was interred at Canterbury and that the Maidstone skeleton is of an imposter — unless, of course, Courtenay was interred at Maidstone in simple fashion and not in full canonicals.

Fancett, William (1815-1918). Centenarian. When he died he was believed to be the oldest man in Kent, at 103. He could remember all but one of Maidstone's churches being built and had canvassed on behalf of Benjamin Disraeli when he stood as M.P. for Maidstone, 1837. On retirement as a traveller for a local brewer he worked in the Salem Street Mission Rooms and did mission work helping the hop-pickers in the local hop gardens, he having been born at East Peckham. Interred in Maidstone Cemetery, in the grave of his wife (d.1876). (See Boughton-under-Blean—Hawkins; Kennington—Parker)

Grocyn, William (d.1519). Renaissance Scholar. Appointed Master of the College of Priests, 1506. Friend of Erasmus. Interred in the chancel of All Saints' Church, Maidstone, but the exact location is unknown.

Norton, Stephen (d.1381). Bellfounder. An example of his bells is in the former Holy Cross Church, Westgate, now Canterbury's council meeting place. It bears the inscription 'Stephanus Nortone de Kent me fecit': 'Stephen Norton of Kent made me'. Reputedly interred in the north aisle of All Saints' Church, Maidstone, but due to the date of his death he was probably interred in the Saxon St Mary's Church that was demolished and rebuilt in 1395 to become All Saints' Church on the site of the earlier church. In 'Joseph Hatch — The Ulcombe Bellfounder' published and printed by John Hilton, Hadlow, the author states: 'In All Saints' Church, Maidstone, is the tomb of Stephen Norton, bellfounder, who was casting bells at the end of the 14th century, although the foundry site is not known'. An ancestor of Alan Major through the latter's maternal grandfather, Joseph Norton of Great Chart.

Sharp, Sir Edward (1854-1931). Founder of Edward Sharp & Co. Ltd., confectioners, makers of the famous 'Kreemy' toffee. Interred in Maidstone Cemetery, Sutton Road, Maidstone.

Shipley, William (1715-1803). Founder of the Royal Society of Arts. His well-maintained table tomb is in the north-west corner of All Saints' Churchyard, Maidstone.

Washington, Lawrence (1546-1619). A member of the Washington family whose descendant was George Washington. By the south door of All Saints' Church, Maidstone, is a memorial tablet which states that he lies nearby. The top of the memorial has the embryonic American flag, with stars and stripes in the Washington heraldic device.

Woodville, Richard (d. between 1440 and 1442). 'Forebear' of Elizabeth, Queen of Edward IV, and her brother Lord Rivers (presumably Anthony, 2nd Lord Rivers, who was patron of Caxton). Esquire of the Body to Henry V, Seneschal of Normandy, Lieutenant of Calais. Interred under an indent in the Sanctuary, north side, in All Saints' Church, Maidstone.

Wotton (Wootton), John (d.1417). First Master of the College of Priests who staffed the Collegiate Church, Maidstone. His canopied tomb is in the south chancel aisle, All Saints' Church, Maidstone.

MARGATE

Fuller, Albert (1891-1948). Entertainer and Concert Party Comedian. As 'Leslie Fuller' he appeared regularly in a Show called 'The Peddlers' at Cliftonville's Lido in the 1920s and 1930s, but he also became a starring actor in cheap film comedies. He made 26 films, starting his film career in 1930 with 'Not So Quiet on the Western Front', while his last film was 'What Do We Do Now?' in 1945. Interred, grave number 7,943, St John's Cemetery, Manston Road, Margate.

Horne, Richard Henry (Hengist) (1801-1884). Author. Poet. Playwright. Editor. After an early nautical career, as Midshipman in the Mexican Navy, he started his literary career writing on these experiences. In 1837 he wrote a tragedy 'The Death of Marlowe'. Corresponded with Elizabeth Barrett before her marriage to Browning. Wrote two children's fiction books: 'The Good Natured Bear' and 'Memoirs of a London Doll', under a pen-name 'Mrs. Fairstar'. While resident in Australia 1852-1869 he called himself Richard Henry Horne but after he met a Mr. Hengist in the Bush he changed his name to Richard Hengist Horne. After his death a mass of unpublished material was found, including the manuscript 'The Great Peace Maker — A Submarine Dialogue on the laying of the submarine cable between Dover and France' which was eventually published. Interred in St John's Cemetery, Manston Road, Margate, grave number 603, the interment being paid for by a James Horne of St John's Wood, London.

Jesse, Emilia (Emily) (1814-1887). Sister of Alfred Lord Tennyson. She was engaged to Arthur Hallam, Tennyson's scholar friend, who taught her Italian and wrote sonnets to her, but he died of apoplexy, 1833. In January, 1842, she married Richard Jesse, a Lieutenant, later Captain, in the Royal Navy. Curiously it was not this wedding that Tennyson used as the symbolic end of his mourning for Hallam and the augury of the future in 'In Memoriam', but that of Cecilia Tennyson and Edmund Lushington in Autumn 1842. Emily rather surprisingly named her first son Arthur Henry Hallam Jesse. She toured Europe and witnessed the revolution in Paris, 1848. As she became older she grew more eccentric and dabbled in spiritualism with her husband. She died at Sweyne Road, Cliftonville, and was interred in grave 1,217, St John's Cemetery, Manston Road, Margate. Mee in his 'Kent' states that she was interred 'side by side' with her sister Mary 'in Margate cemetery'. Mary (see below) was interred in grave number 830.

Ker, Mary (1811-1884). Sister of Alfred Lord Tennyson. Unexpectedly, without notice to her family, she married Alan Ker, then a penniless Cheltenham barrister, which caused Tennyson to comment that he had done so to get himself more soundly financially launched on a career. Like her sister Emily she became a convinced spiritualist later in life. Died at Dalby Road, Cliftonville, and was interred in grave 830, St John's Cemetery, Manston Road, Margate. (See Boxley—Tennyson; Margate—Jesse)

Sanger, 'Lord' George (1825-1911). Circus Proprietor and Showman. Youngest son of James Sanger (d.1850), a naval pensioner who served on the *Victory* at Trafalgar, later becoming a showman. Brother of 'Lord' John Sanger (see below). First appeared as a performer on the day of Queen Victoria's Coronation, 1838. In 1845 he joined his brother in a conjuring act, then they, with their other brother William, started their own 'show' at Stepney Fair. George about this time was the first to introduce the naphtha lamp to London. In 1853 he and John started a modest circus and travelling show, that gradually grew until it outrivalled any American and European circus. He bought a hall at Ramsgate for winter circus spectaculars, his head-quarters being the Hall-by-the-Sea, Margate, where he also housed wild animals in the walls of what later became part of the grounds of Dreamland. About 1871 he dissolved the partnership with John, whom he outpaced for enterprise, showmanship and public fame. In 1887 he took the 'title' of 'Lord' to combat that of 'Hon.' William Cody (Buffalo Bill). In 1887 he also founded the Showman's Guild and was president for 18 years. He sold his circus in 1905, and published his autobiography 'Seventy Years A Showman' in 1910. In 1850 he had married Ellen Chapman (d.1899), a lion tamer who performed till marriage with Wombwell's Menagerie as 'Madame Pauline de Vere'. They had one son who died before his father, and a daughter Harriet Reeve. He was interred by the side of his wife, with municipal honours, in St John's Cemetery, Manston Road, Margate, his grave adjoining that of his brother John and having prominent angels at each corner. He was not shot, as news-papers claimed, by his former valet and attendant, Herbert Cooper, who committed suicide, but, according to his grandson, George Sanger Coleman, in

A pre-1914 postcard view of the grave and memorial of the nine men drowned when the Margate surf boat 'Friend to All Nations' capsized in December 1897. Published by A.W. Elkin, 24 Marine Terrace, Margate, presumably while this disaster was still fresh in local people's memory. The main difference to this view today is that the trees are much higher and at the base of the memorial, instead of what appears to be a turf cross, are clipped evergreen shrubs. The memorial has recently been restored.

(Postcard in author's collection)

his 'The Sanger Story', 1956, George Sanger received an unlucky blow with a candlestick when he tried to intervene in a quarrel.

Sanger, 'Lord' John (1816-1889). Circus Proprietor and Showman. Eldest son of James Sanger who had been seized by a press gang to serve on the *Victory*. He leased the Agricultural Hall, Islington, and, after he and George dissolved their partnership in 1871, Astley's Amphitheatre, London. His company toured in summer and put on spectacles in London in winter. His first equestrian pantomime at Astley's was 'Lady Godiva or Harlequin St. George and the Dragon', 1871. He took the 'title' of 'Lord' at about the same time as his brother George. He had three sons: John, who continued the circus business, George Lord, and James; also a daughter, Lavinia, Mrs Hoffman, an equestrian performer. Interred in St John's Cemetery, Manston Road, Margate, beneath a large white marble monument bearing the name Sanger in capitals and various equestrian motifs. It is surmounted by an almost life-size mourning circus horse that can easily be seen across the Cemetery. Other members of the Sanger family are interred in close proximity, including 'Lord' George Sanger.

Whitten, Wilfred (1864-1942). Journalist. Known as 'John O'London'. Editor of 'John O'London's Weekly', 1919-1936. Interred in grave number 13,813, Unconsecrated section, St John's Cemetery, Manston Road, Margate.

87

Ymar, Saint (d.830). Monk of the Order of Saint Benedict. Martyred by the Danes by burning, at Reculver. He was interred in 'the Church of St John Thanet', his body being translated after 1050 to St John's Church, Margate, the site of his tomb reputedly being by the font. The coffin stone is still preserved in the church.

Lifeboatmen's Grave. On December 2nd, 1897, the Margate surf boat *Friend to All Nations* capsized when attempting to assist a ship in distress. Nine men on the surf boat were drowned. They were interred beneath a large, recently restored memorial with nautical motifs, in St John's Cemetery, Manston Road, Margate. On one side a tablet records 'This Memorial was erected at the expense of the Fund so generously subscribed by the public. It was unveiled in the presence of the Committee, Widows and their Families, 25th April 1900'. The names of the victims are also stated around the Memorial: William Philpott Cook, Snr., aged 54, Coxwain; his son, William Philpott Cook, Jnr., aged 28; Robert Ernest Cook, aged 26; Edward Robert Crunden, aged 31; William Richard Gill, aged 36; John Benjamin Dike, aged 41; George Robert William Ladd, aged 38 and Henry Richard Brockman, aged 50; all these were crew members. The ninth man was Charles E. Troughton, Superintendent of Margate Ambulance Corps. On Margate seafront overlooking the Parade there is a statue of a lifeboatman of that period erected in their memory which also lists all their names.

MEOPHAM

Bayley, Sir John (1763-1841). Judge. Recorder of Maidstone who sat as Judge of the King's Bench for 22 years. Judge in the action for libel in 1819 brought by the Attorney-General against Richard Carlile for re-publishing Thomas Paine's 'Age of Reason'. He married Elizabeth Markett of Meopham Court Lodge and was interred in the chancel of St John the Baptist Church, Meopham.

MEREWORTH

Fane, Sir Thomas (d.1589). Politician. He was involved in Wyatt's Rebellion, 1554, committed to the Tower of London and sentenced to death but surprisingly Mary I took pity on him because of his youth and ordered his release. He was knighted in Dover Castle, 1573, in the presence of Elizabeth I. In 1580 he was appointed Deputy Commissioner with the task of increasing and breeding horses in Kent and for the keeping of horses and geldings ready for service with the Crown's forces. When the Armada was expected he did good service deploying forces along the Kent coast to defend it. He was first interred in Tudeley Church, then, according to the 'Dictionary of National Biography', was removed to St Laurence's Church, Mereworth, where, on his second marriage, he had come into possession of the Castle and Manor of Mereworth. (Not to be confused with the Sir Thomas Fane, a member of the same family, interred in a tomb in Hunton Church).

Hall, Sir William Hutcheon (1797?-1878). Admiral. Known in the Royal Navy as 'Nemesis' Hall, since he commanded the iron paddle-steamer *Nemesis* on the India and China Stations, 1839-1843. He later commanded the paddle-steamer *Hecla* in the Crimean War. It was on this vessel that C.D. Lucas (see below), serving as Mate, won the Victoria Cross on 21st June 1854. Lucas married Hall's daughter in 1879. In 1852 Hall published 'Sailors' Homes, their Origin & Progress' and in 1876 'Our National Defences'. He is interred in St Laurence's Churchyard, Mereworth.

Lucas, Charles Davis (1834-1914). The First Winner of the Victoria Cross. He won it while serving as a 20 year old Mate on H.M.S. *Hecla* in the Baltic during the Crimean War. On 21st June 1854, when a live enemy shell landed on the deck he picked it up and threw it overboard where it exploded, thus saving many of the crew's lives and possibly the ship. This was even more heroic when it is realised that this type of shell was filled with explosive and had a short time fuse set to explode a few seconds after impact. He was promoted to Lieutenant on the spot and later rose to the rank of Admiral. When it was instituted on 29th January 1856, at the close of the Crimean War, Charles Lucas was awarded the first V.C. He received it personally from Queen Victoria, as did 61 others, in Hyde Park on 26th June 1857. Also receiving his V.C. that day was another Kent man, Joseph Kellaway (see Chatham—Kellaway). Lucas is interred in St Laurence's Churchyard, Mereworth.

MERSHAM
Knatchbull, Sir Norton (d.1636). Sheriff of Kent, 1608. M.P. for Hythe, 1609. Founder of Ashford Free Grammar School. Interred in the chancel of St John's Church, Mersham.

MILTON-BY-GRAVESEND
Wyatt, Sir Henry (d. 1537). Soldier. Politician. Father of the poet Sir Thomas Wyatt (1503-1542). He resisted Richard III's path to the throne of England and was arrested and imprisoned in the Tower of London. Here Richard witnessed Wyatt put on the rack and having vinegar and mustard forced down his throat. On Richard's orders he was then to be left to die of starvation and cold, but there is a legend that while Wyatt was in the Tower a cat came and slept on his chest at night to keep him warm and brought him a pigeon every day from a nearby dovecot, thus saving him from starvation. On the north choir wall of the chancel of Boxley Church is a memorial that relates this. There does not, however, appear to be any written confirmation of such an event, although in 1727 when the Wyatt family papers were drawn up it was noted that Sir Henry, on his release, 'would ever make much of cats, as other men will of their spaniels or hounds', so there may be some truth in the story. He was freed on the accession of Henry VII, made a Privy Councillor and appointed Guardian of the young Henry VIII. On becoming king Henry VIII treated Wyatt with favour, making him a Knight of the Bath in 1509,

and Treasurer to the King's Chamber in 1524. In 1492 he had bought Allington Castle and its estates, and Henry VIII visited him there. In accordance with his last wishes he was interred in St Peter & St Paul's Church, Milton-by-Gravesend. (See Boxley—both Wyatts)

MILTON REGIS

Gilker, Simon (1648-1696). Possibly the First Firework Casualty in England. The inscription on his headstone reads: 'who was killed by means of a rockett November 5th 1696 aged 48'. Gilker was Churchwarden (then Administrator of the Poor Law). The circumstances that caused his death are unknown, possibly the carelessness of others or accident. In the opinion of the Vicar of Milton Regis, Rev. W. Drury, 'If one assumes that Bonfire Night as we know it came in only with the Restoration in 1660 (before 1640 it had more the aura of a between-wars Remembrance Day, and Cromwellian England would not have observed it at all) Mr. Gilker must have been one of the earliest casualties. The 'rockett', presumably a ship's signal rocket, would have been 'liberated' from the Navy at Sheerness, one imagines'. Milton was also a staunchly royalist and busy port, so the 'rockett' may have come from there and gone off-course. The date of death indicates the 'rockett' was part of a Gunpowder Plot Commemmoration, but whether the 'rockett' came from a naval source or from a local event, a royalist party, is unknown. Gilker may have attended such an event in an official capacity but it is unlikely he was personally involved with setting off 'rocketts', more likely an unlucky witness. Interred immediately across the path from the church porch, Holy Trinity with St Paul's Churchyard, Milton Regis.

Norton, Sir John (d.1534). Sheriff of Kent, 1514, during the reign of Henry VIII. Interred in an altar tomb in the Sanctuary of the Norwood Chapel, Holy Trinity with St Paul's Church, Milton Regis.

MINSTER-IN-SHEPPEY

Cheney (Cheyne, Cheyney), Sir Thomas (1485-1558/9). Sheriff of Kent, 1516. Squire of the Body to Henry VIII, 1519. Lord Warden of the Cinque Ports, 1536. Henry VIII's Deputy in Paris at the christening of Henry III of France, 1546. He was involved in supporting Mary I against Wyatt's Rebellion, 1554. Privy Councillor to Mary and Elizabeth. He demolished some of Chilham Castle and used the stone to build Shurland Castle, Sheppey which was visited by Henry VIII and Anne Boleyn in 1532. Tomb and effigy stand beneath the organ loft in St Mary & St Sexburga's Church, Minster-in-Sheppey, to which it was moved in 1581 when St Katherine's Chapel was demolished by Sir Humphrey Gilbert.

de Shurland, Sir Robert (d.1310?). He took part in the Crusade of 1271 with Prince Edward, later Edward I, who created him Knight Banneret for gallantry against the Scots at the Siege of Carlaverock, 1301. Lord Warden of the Cinque Ports, with privilege of 'wreck of the sea' on his lands, meaning that his jurisdiction extended to anything a man could touch with his lance after riding as far as possible into the sea at low tide. This may account for the horse's head that appears to be rising from waves behind the sleeping knight on his tomb. Alternatively it may commemorate a favourite animal on which he is claimed to have crossed the nearby Swale. There is also the well-known whimsical tale concerning the horse's head in Rev. Richard Barham's 'The Grey Dolphin' in the 'Ingoldsby Legends'. An unusual feature of Shurland's tomb is the figure of his page or esquire lying at his feet, instead of a hound or cushion. Interred in the south chancel of the Abbey Church, St Mary & St Sexburga's, Minster-in-Sheppey.

MINSTER-IN-THANET

Lewis, John (1675-1747). Author. Vicar of Margate, 1705; Rector of Saltwood and Hythe, 1706; Vicar of Minster-in-Thanet, 1708. He wrote books on topography and biography, three being on Caxton, Wycliff and Bishop John Fisher. He also edited Roper's 'Life of More', 1729 (see Canterbury—Roper). His topographical books such as 'The History and Antiquities, Ecclesiastical and Civil, of the Isle of Tenet in Kent', 1723, and 'The History and Antiquities of the Abbey and Church of Faversham, the Prior of Davington and Maison-dieu, Ospringe in Kent', 1727 are more important. He also wrote books on religious history and bibliography, and antiquarian and theological tracts. Interred in the chancel of St Mary's Church, Minster-in-Thanet.

MONGEHAM

St Leger, Edward (1666-1729). Surgeon at Deal. His tomb in the north chapel of St Martin's Church, Great Mongeham, has a glowing inscription relating his many virtues: 'Mr Edward St Leger, descended from a Family of Great Honour and Antiquity, the Founder of it being Sr. Robert De Santo Leodegario, who came with William the Conqueror and settled at Ulcombe . . . his descendants were eminent in war, as well as peace, for we read of several judges, generals, knights of ye garter, lord deputies of Ireland and knight bannerets against them . . . Thus was this gentleman descended but . . . inherited only the virtues of his ancestors. For in the 40 years he took care of the sick and wounded at Deal it was hard to say whether his fidelity to his government, his ? or his humanity to the unhappy sufferers were more conspicuous, nor were his private virtues less than his public. For in him is lost a most intelligent husband, a tender father, a kind relation, a good master and a faithful friend; such was Mr St Leger'. It seems he was also one of the very few people who could genuinely claim descent from the Norman invaders of Kent in 1066.

MONKS HORTON

Robinson-Morris, Matthew (1713-1800). 2nd Baron Rokeby. Eccentric. Through his mother he inherited the Morris estates at Horton near Hythe and took the surname of Morris. M.P. for Canterbury, 1747 and 1754, though due to ill-health he withdrew from Parliament but continued his interest in politics. Between 1774 and 1777 he published four pamphlets against the Government's American policy and in 1797 an 'Address to the County of Kent' advising dismissal of Pitt. Canterbury Library Archives possess a copy. He was said to have been 'the only peer of his day who wore a beard'. He lived mainly on beef tea and was an enthusiastic drinker of water, but he abhorred fires. He had a bath so constructed that it was warmed by the sun's rays and he passed many hours in it. He refused all medical advice and is said to have threatened to cut off his nephew-heir from his Will if the latter called a doctor during one of his fits. He understood the theory and practice of grazing and much of his estate was laid with grass. He was generous with the tenants on his estate and in character was said at times to be 'whimsical'. He took long walks that would have tired a horse. One of his sisters was Mrs Elizabeth Montagu, authoress and society hostess for fifty years in London and Tunbridge Wells. Robinson-Morris died at his seat 'Mount Morris' on 30th November 1800 and, according to the 'Dictionary of National Biography', was interred 'at Monks Horton' (St Peter's Church) on 8th December 1800.

NEWCHURCH

Cole, Barney (1835-1922). Rock Breaker. He worked by the roadside with hammers breaking down large rocks to smaller sizes for use in road mending, and wore eccentric clothing while he did so. Interred in St Peter & St Paul's Churchyard, Newchurch. The grave is unmarked, but the position is shown on the churchyard plan.

NEWINGTON-NEXT-SITTINGBOURNE

le Bouser, Robert (d.early 12th century). Murder Victim. A pilgrim en route to Canterbury, he was murdered on Watling Street. His tomb was reputedly the scene of many miraculous cures. It is a table tomb with four arches, one of which is open. It was claimed that if anyone infirm or ill crawled through the open space or put the affected limb in it the infirmity or disease would be cured. The tomb is in the Lady Chapel, St Mary the Virgin's Church, Newington-next-Sittingbourne. Other murder victims are at Hoath, Ightham, Hoo St Werburgh and Southborough.

NEW ROMNEY

Stuppenye, Richard (d.1526). Jurat of New Romney. Around his table tomb at the east end of the south aisle of St Nicholas' Church, the Jurats of Romney (New Romney being a Cinque Port) assembled annually to elect their new Mayor. The inscription reads: 'Here lyeth buried the body of Richard Stuppenye, Jurat of this town in the first year of King Henry VIII who died in the XVIII year of the said king's reign of whose memory Clement Stuppenye of the same port (see Lydd) his great-grandson has caused the tomb to be new erected for the use of the ancient meeting and election of mayor and jurats of the port town June 10th anno dm 1622.' A 19th century Act of Parliament, The Municipal Corporations Act, stopped such customs in churches.

Triplets' Death. A grave slab inscription in St Nicholas' Church, New Romney, reads: 'Here lyeth the body of William Willcocke, son of Robert Willcocke, as also the bodies of his three sons William, John and Robert posthumous of his wife, Elizabeth, who lived together in their mother's womb, And dying so lie in their father's tomb. He died April 7th, in the 24th year of his age, 1642. They died June 26, 27, 28, in the first week of theirs, AD.1642.' (See Westbere—Jenkins)

NORTHBOURNE

Sandys, Sir Edwin (1561-1629). Traveller. Member of James I's first Parliament. He was appointed Member of the Council of Virginia, 1607, but displeased the king in 1620 and was not re-elected. Instead he was imprisoned in the Tower of London, but in 1621 was elected as M.P. for Sandwich. In later years he served the East India Company. Interred in St Augustine's Church, Northbourne, near Deal. (See Boxley—Sandys)

NORTHFLEET

Ekman, Carl Daniel (1845-1904). Pioneer Research Scientist for the Paper Industry. He came to Northfleet from Sweden, 1879, and founded The Ekman Pulp & Paper Company, erecting a mill in 1883. At first the company was profitable but by the late 1890s there were various financial problems, including rising costs of research and a lawsuit against the company. He had experimented with and succeeded in bleaching mechanical paper pulp to establish the sulphite pulp industry. The lawsuit was brought because some sulphite waste had penetrated a limestone quarry causing the formation of sulphurous acid. The strain of the lawsuit and an attack of typhoid fever resulted in his death at his home, The Laurels, Overcliffe, Gravesend. Interred in St Botolph's Churchyard, Northfleet. Until October 1934 his grave was unmarked, but a memorial of Swedish black granite was then erected and unveiled by the Swedish Cellulose Association.

NORTON

Lushington, Stephen Rumbold (1776-1868). Indian Official. Private Secretary to 1st Lord Harris when C. in C. Madras, 1795-1799, and also Civil Administrator. Governor of Madras, 1827-1835. M.P. for Canterbury, 1835-1837. His first wife was Anne, eldest daughter of Lord Harris, conqueror of Seringapatam, 1815. In 1840 he published the 'Life' of his father-in-law. Interred in St Mary's Church, Norton. (See Boxley—Lushington; Sittingbourne—Lushington)

The very tall headstone to James Baldwin
at Orpington.   (Photograph by
courtesy of Kenneth Miller, Beckenham)

OLD ROMNEY

Deffray, John (d.1738). Rector of Old Romney for almost 48 years. One of the thousands of French Protestants driven from France who came to England as skilled refugees after the Revocation of the Edict of Nantes that had given freedom of worship. It states in the register 'he took possession of the rectory on 10th August 1690, after reading prayers and the Thirty-Nine Articles'. Interred beneath a memorial ledger stone in the centre of the chancel floor, St Clement's Church, Old Romney.

ORPINGTON

Baldwin, James (1764-1844). Woodreeve (a person whose duties are the care and maintenance of woodland). His epitaph, an example of 19th century snobbery and condescension, reads: 'He was an industrious and inoffensive man and served Lady Glode many years and Mr James Glode Stapleton twenty years as woodreeve. Mr Stapleton has erected this stone to mark worth and diligence in humble life. "Jesus said unto her, I am the resurrection and the life, he that believeth in me though he was dead, yet shall he live and whosoever liveth and believeth in me shall never die". Reader, believeth thou this?' An exceptionally tall headstone, about 6 feet high above ground marks his grave in All Saints' Churchyard, Orpington.

OTHAM

Stevens, William (1732-1807). 'Nobody'. A Hosier and bachelor who, as a partner in a firm in Old Broad Street, London, amassed a fortune. He retired in 1801 to devote himself to literary studies, giving away his money periodically to various causes. He learnt French, Latin, Greek and Hebrew and was the biographer and editor of the works of William Jones of Nayland, leader of a section of churchmen forming a link between the nonjurors and the Oxford tractarians. He founded a 'Society for the Reformation of Principles', to counteract the influence of the French Revolution, the Society publishing several of his tracts for young clergy. His main study was theology and he published several volumes of sermons, religious translations and essays on religious subjects. He gave financial support to church societies and the work to improve the episcopal church in Scotland. In the 'British Critic' he published a defence of his cousin, George Horne, later Bishop of Norwich, and in 'Strictures on a Sermon' attacked Richard Watson, Professor of Divinity, Cambridge. Certainly not the actions of a shy, timid man, as his character has so often been described. He wrote 'Letters on Infidelity' and for this and his articles and other books he used the pseudonym 'Ain', Hebrew for 'Nobody'. In 1800 a club that met three times a year was founded in his honour by his friends, called 'Nobody's Works'. Numbers were restricted to fifty members from all walks of life, their only link being that they knew Stevens. A collection of his tracts was issued in 1805 with the title 'Nobody's Works'. After his death the club continued in his memory but as 'Nobody's Friends' and is still in existence. He left most of his property to his cousin, William Horne, Rector of Otham. Interred in St Nicholas' Churchyard, Otham, close to the wall beside the road. There is a memorial tablet in the church, and a new stone (its inscription now largely illegible) was erected by the Society in 1890. (See Biddenden—Nares)

PENSHURST

Gort, Viscount John Standish Surtees Prendergast Vereker (1886-1946). Field Marshal. Victoria Cross Winner, also D.S.O., M.C., G.C.B., K.C.B. Won his V.C. during service in the First World War, 1918. In the Second World War he was Commander-in-Chief 1939-40 of the British Forces overwhelmed by German victories in France and Belgium. A.D.C. to George VI, 1940-1944. Governor of Malta, 1942-1944. High Commissioner for Palestine, 1944-1945. Related by marriage to the Sidney family, father-in-law of Lord de Lisle of Penshurst. Interred in a vault in St John the Baptist's Church, Penshurst.

Sidney, Algernon (1622-1683). Soldier. Political Writer. Served with distinction in Cromwell's army, but refused to take part in government, although he acted as a Council of State member. On the Restoration of Charles II he went into exile for 17 years, but returned to Kent on receiving

The mysteriously inscribed headstone of Thomas Crafts with the surname underlined by a snake and the figure 7 upside down, in All Saints' Churchyard, Petham.
(Photograph by the author)

permission to live again at Penshurst. On the discovery of the Rye House Plot he was accused of treason and sent to the Tower on a very weak charge. Brought to trial before notorious Judge Jeffreys, with no evidence except that of the traitor Lord Howard and his own unpublished 'Discourses', he was not allowed to defend himself and due to his association with the Parliamentary Goverment was found guilty and beheaded on Tower Hill. His 'Discourses Concerning Government' was published posthumously in 1698. Interred in the Sidney Chapel, St John the Baptist's Church, Penshurst.

Sidney, Sir Henry (1529-1586). Lord Deputy of Ireland. Edward VI died in his arms. Supported the cause of Lady Jane Grey, but when Mary I was proclaimed Queen he changed sides and though disliked for being a turncoat managed to escape punishment. Despite this he went to Spain in connection with the marriage between Philip and Mary, his eldest son being named Philip after the king who was his godfather. On Mary's death Elizabeth confirmed him in his Irish office but he eventually fell from favour and was banished from her court. He died at Ludlow Castle where his heart was interred, but on Elizabeth's orders his body was interred in the Sidney Chapel, St John the Baptist's Church, Penshurst.

Sidney, Margaret (d.1558). Infant daughter of Sir Henry Sidney (1529-1586). Interred in the Sidney Chapel, St John the Baptist's Church, Penshurst, notable because the site bears a brass stating that she died in the reign of 'King Philip and Queen Mary'. Philip was King of Spain and thought of in some quarters as King of England through his marriage to Mary in 1554.

Sidney, Sir William (1482?-1553/4?). Soldier. Diplomat. Squire of the Body to Henry VIII, he accompanied Henry to the Field of Cloth of Gold, 1520. Interred in the Sidney Chapel, St John the Baptist's Church, Penshurst, in an altar tomb with a memorial tablet bearing engravings of the escutcheons of his four daughters and their husbands. A descendant, Henry Sidney, Earl of Romney (1641-1704), Lord Lieutenant of Kent, 1689-1692 and 1694-1704, brother of Algernon Sidney, while Master-General of the Ordnance, 1693-94, first used the altar tomb's 'pheon' or 'broad arrow' as the mark for Government property. Henry is interred in St James's Church, Piccadilly.

PETHAM

On the south side of the chancel of All Saints' Church, Petham, in the old churchyard, is the grave of **Thomas Crafts,** who died on 15th February 1807, aged 68 years. Curiously the 7 in the year is cut upside down as L. Another oddity is that the surname Crafts is underlined with what looks like a long straight snake. More Crafts family members are interred alongside but have normal lettering and no 'snake'. (See Benenden—Drury)

PLUCKLEY

Board, John William (1821-1850). Stationmaster at Pluckley, 'killed in the execution of his duty', 7th November 1850. Also his wife, Jane (1822-1875) for 24 years 'ladies' attendant' at Dover Station, much respected by all who knew her. Both interred on east side of St Nicholas' Church, Pluckley. (See Ashford—Wainwright)

Handley, Henry (1796-1846). A Founder of the Royal Agricultural Society of England. M.P. for Lincolnshire, his home was Culverthorpe Hall, Lincolnshire, but he died at Surrenden-Dering. Interred in an altar tomb in St Nicholas' Churchyard, Pluckley.

Hugo, Miss Grace (1782-1872). 'Died in full possession of all her faculties in the 90th year of her age'. Perhaps she lived to this great age because she was not married! (See Pluckley—Rucke) Interred on the east side of St Nicholas' Churchyard, Pluckley.

Nepecker, Edward (1690-1720). 'Dyed of ye smallpox', aged 30. Interred on east side of St Nicholas' Churchyard, Pluckley. (See Hothfield—Stanford; Lydd—Austin; Sundridge—Mompesson)

Norden, Thomas (no dates on gravestone but burial register states that he was buried May 1717). The epitaph is worth reading but does not say much for the other people living at that time in Pluckley! 'He pleased God and was beloved of Him so that living among sinners he was translated. Yea speedily was he taken away lest that wickedness should alter his understanding or deceit beguile his soul. He being made perfect in a short time fulfilled a long time. For his soul pleased the Lord therefore hasted He to take him away from among the wicked.' There is a similar theme inscription on a tomb on the left of the path from the war memorial to the church porch in Farningham Churchyard: 'God takes the good, too good on earth to stay, And leaves the bad, too bad to take away'. Norden is interred close to the tower, St Nicholas' Churchyard, Pluckley.

Rucke, Mary (1749-1799). 'Died aged 50 after a few days illness having been married only 15 days.' It would seem married life did not suit this longtime spinster! Interred on the north side of St Nicholas' Churchyard, Pluckley. (See Pluckley—Hugo)

Spicer, Jesse (1745-1772). His gravestone, east of the church, states: 'In Memory of Jesse Spicer killed by a Ninepin Bowl . . . aged 27'. The accident(?) happened at the Black Horse Inn, Pluckley. Not to be confused with descendants also named Jesse Spicer in the same St Nicholas' Churchyard, Pluckley.

RAINHAM

Chambers, John (d.1767). On the south side of the tower of Rainham Church is a tomb unlike others in the churchyard, although it is a style seen elsewhere. The base is made of bricks on which lies a six inch thick oblong slab of limestone upon which is another of similar shape and thickness. Upon the latter is a coffin-shaped limestone slab in two sections and placed on this an upright stone of limestone bearing an almost illegible inscription. At the summit is a three-feet high flat-topped spire. There is a local legend concerning how and why this tomb was thus shaped. It is reputed that John Chambers was on the top of the church tower when he leaned too far over and fell to his death below. He landed on his head which became so wedged in the soft earth it was impossible to pull him out. So his relatives ordered a local mason to build the tomb around the upright lifeless body of Chambers. One wonders, however, why they did not dig around his head to release him! A legend says that if you walk around the tomb seven times carrying a needle on an out-stretched hand (another version says you must also drop the needle at the end of the seventh revolution) you will hear John Chambers groaning for help. As a child I tried it — nothing happened. Also interred in the grave is his wife Elizabeth (d.1776) (see Farningham—Mausoleum game, also 7 curiosity Crafts—Petham). (An alternative version says if anyone runs around the grave seven times carrying a pin or needle they will hear the angry Devil down below.) Another legend suggests the Devil was on a visit to Rainham, found the church tower door open and to gain entrance to the church climbed the

The grave of John Chambers with its 'devil' association and other curious beliefs in St Margaret's Churchyard, Rainham.   (Photograph by the author)

stairs to the top of the tower. This is supposed to have occurred on bell-ringing practice evening, and unknown to him the ringers had followed behind and started to ring the bells. To get away from the din he leapt over the tower parapet and landed with a heavy fall on top of Chambers' tomb, breaking the top off it so it is blunt today. There is a similar legend at nearby Newington-next-Sittingbourne.

Cobb, Rev. Charles (1828-1918). Albert Medal Winner. Sea Rescue Hero. In January 1867 the French ship *Courrier de Dieppe* went aground and was being pounded by heavy seas. Charles Cobb, then Vicar of Dymchurch, went into the sea with a coastguard, John Batist, and together they rescued the sole survivor of the four-man crew, the mate Vincent Mariere. Next day he had the task of burying one of the drowned crew who had been washed ashore. For his bravery he was awarded the Albert Medal, 1st Class (For Gallantry in Saving Life at Sea). He also was awarded the Gold Medal of the Royal Humane Society; the Gold Medal of the Royal National Lifeboat Institution and a medal by the French Emperor Napoleon III. Batist was awarded the Albert Medal, 2nd Class, similarly inscribed. A copy of Cobb's citation for the award is displayed in Dymchurch Church. In 1876 he became Vicar of Rainham and held the incumbency until he resigned, the vacancy being filled by his son-in-law, Rev. J.M. Tamplin. Cobb resided at the vicarage Rainham, until he died. Interred in St Margaret's Churchyard, Rainham, on the east side of the chancel, facing Church Path. The stone, though having names and dates, fails to give any clue that a hero is interred there. Similarly the plaque in the church recording his 32 years as Vicar of Rainham does not mention the sea rescue, nor does it, or the gravestone, include the letters A.M. after his name that he was entitled to use as holder of the Albert Medal.

RAMSGATE

Montefiore, Sir Moses (1784-1885). Philanthropist. High Sheriff of Kent. In 1833 he built a Jewish synagogue in the hamlet of Hereson. Adjoining the synagogue he also built a mausoleum in the style of the Tomb of Rachel in Jerusalem. His wife, Lady Judith Montefiore, died in 1862 and to perpetuate her memory he had built in 1869 the Judith Lady Montefiore College. On his death aged 101 he was laid to rest with his wife in the mausoleum.

Pugin, Augustus Welby (1812-1852). Architect. He loved Gothic architecture and promoted its revival in his own work. He assisted Barry in designing the new Houses of Parliament, especially the interior fittings and decorations. In 1834 he became a Roman Catholic. He came to live in Ramsgate in 1843 and built 'The Grange' on West Cliff. Next to it he built St Augustine's Church at his own expense and there he was eventually interred.

RIPPLE

French, John Denton Pinkston (1852-1925). 1st Earl of Ypres. Field Marshal. C-in-C, British Forces in France, 1914-1915. C-in-C Home Forces, 1915-1918. Interred in St Mary the Virgin's Churchyard, Ripple. There are memorials to earlier members of the French family in the church.

ROCHESTER

Gundulf (1025?-1108). Bishop of Rochester. Architect. Rebuilt the cathedral church. William the Conqueror employed him to build the Tower of London including the White Tower. He was interred by Anselm in the cathedral. The tomb said to be his lies on the south side of the choir, near the altar. This is really of the 15th century, though perhaps it may contain his body.

de Merton, Walter (d.1277). Bishop. Founder of Merton College, Oxford. His tomb has an Elizabethan effigy in alabaster. Interred in a tomb under a window in the north choir transept, Rochester Cathedral.

de Sheppey, John (d.1360). Bishop. His tomb with its coloured effigy is sited between St John's Chapel and the Presbytery at the east end of Rochester Cathedral and was discovered in the wall in 1825.

Watts, Richard (1529-1579). Founder of Watts Charity, Rochester. Contractor for the Government, 1550-1551, paid for victualling the fleet and army. In 1560 Elizabeth I appointed him Paymaster and Surveyor of Works, Upnor Castle, then in 1562 Surveyor of the Ordnance, Upnor. In 1573 he was visited at his house in Rochester by Elizabeth on her 'Progress' through Kent. There is a story that as she was leaving he apologised for the insufficiency of his house and his entertainment of her, but she remarked 'Satis' (satisfactory, sufficient). He took this as a compliment and named the house, on Boley Hill, 'Satis House', where he died. By his Will he founded the almshouse in Rochester for the relief of the poor: for reception of six poor travellers every night and for 'imploying' the poor of the city. It was Charles Dickens who urged reform of the Charity in the Christmas edition of 'Household Words' in 1854. It was remodelled in 1859 and twenty almsfolk were also lodged in a new building on the Maidstone Road. He was interred in Rochester Cathedral where he asked in his Will: 'neare unto the Steeple and Staires going up into the Quire on the South side of the same Staires . . .' A bust of him, possibly carved in his life-time, surmounts the memorial monument erected in the south transept in 1736.

William of Perth, Saint (d.1201?) A Scottish Baker. On a pilgrimage to Canterbury he was murdered outside Rochester city wall. As he had been a charitable man giving every tenth loaf to the poor the monks buried him in the 'choir' of their cathedral church. Miracles were ascribed to him in his tomb and pilgrims flocked to the shrine. It is reputed that at this time his body was translated to the north choir transept, which became known as the Chapel of St William of Perth. All that survives today of William's supposed tomb is the marble slab top in St John's Chapel removed at some time from the centre of the transept.

RUCKINGE

Ransley, James and William (executed 1800). Smugglers. Known as the 'Rascally Brothers'. Cousins of George Ransley, 'Captain Batts', Smuggler, deported to Tasmania, 1827. The two brothers turned from smuggling to highway robbery at gunpoint and killing if necessary. Finally caught, they were tried, then hanged at Penenden Heath. Their bodies were returned to Ruckinge where they were interred in St Mary Magdalene's Churchyard, near the south door. Reputedly a rough wooden plank with no inscription on three iron supports marks their grave. Nearby a bank called Ransley Green also commemorates them. (See Aldington—Quested)

RYARSH

Larking, Lambert Blackwell (1797-1868). Antiquary. Vicar of Ryarsh from 1830, and also of Burham from 1837, until he died. Hon. Secretary, Kent Archaeological Society from its foundation in 1857 until 1861. He contributed to 'Archaeologica Cantiana'. His translation of 'The Domesday Book of Kent', to which he added notes and an appendix, was published posthumously in 1869. Interred in St Martin's Churchyard, Ryarsh.

The grave of Kentish Samson, Richard Joy, in St Peter's-in-Thanet Churchyard. (Photograph by the author)

The grave of William Cook and his wife Jane in the old sector, Star Lane Cemetery, St Mary Cray. (Photograph by courtesy of A.G. Turner, Petts Wood)

ST MARY CRAY

Cook, William (1849-1904). Poultry Breeder. Bred the famous Black Orpington, White Orpington, Buff Orpington and Speckled Orpington Chickens and the Blue and Buff Orpington Ducks. In 1890 he moved from Orpington to Waldens Manor, St Mary Cray, which he re-named Orpington House. Here he bred the Diamond Jubilee Orpington Chicken in 1897, some examples of which were accepted by Queen Victoria. He published 'W. Cooke's Poultry Breeder & Feeder', 1882 and in 1886 founded 'The Poultry Journal', which he edited. When he widened his interests, even as far as expanding his business to South Africa and America which he visited for the purpose, his eldest daughter, Elizabeth Jane (d.1933) ran the poultry business in Kent and even raised two new chicken breeds in 1907, the Cuckoo Orpington and the Blue Orpington. Tragically, while Cook and his family were visiting the home of a son, William Henry Cook, who was a poultry farmer at Elm Cottage (now Elmdene) St Mary Cray, on 25th June 1903, William Cook's wife Jane was killed in a gas explosion. On the annivesary of her death a year later William Cook died at Skegness while on a short holiday to improve his poor health. Interred with his wife Jane in the old sector, Star Lane Cemetery, St Mary Cray.

102

ST MARY-IN-THE-MARSH

Nesbit, Edith (Mrs Hubert Bland, Mrs Tucker) (1858-1924). Author of children's stories and books, including 'The Railway Children'. The curious marble tomb of Sir John Fagge and his son at Brenzett (see Brenzett—Fagge) was used in one of her ghost stories. Interred on the south side of the churchyard at St Mary-in-the-Marsh Church, Romney Marsh. The grave is marked by a simple wood graveboard carved by her second husband, Captain Tucker.

ST PETER'S-IN-THANET

Joy, Richard (1675-1742). The 'Kentish Samson'. A Strong Man. Naval Seaman. Smuggler. He was able to perform feats of strength, such as lifting a ship's cannon from the port to starboard side and breaking a rope that would take the strain of 35 cwt. On one occasion a rope secured around his waist was tied to the harness of a carthorse and then, hands free of the rope, Joy pulled the horse backwards. He performed his feats in public and also before King George and his family, but could not secure enough income from it. He therefore added to it by becoming a smuggler, and was supposedly drowned on a smuggling run in 1734, but this was a deliberate rumour put about to throw local Revenue Men off the scent. He was eventually caught, but the King heard about it and, learning of the reason for Joy's downfall and remembering the Strong Man of Kent's performances, he suggested sentencing Joy to serve a period of time in the Navy, which he did, putting his strength to good use. Interred near the entrance gate to St Peter's Churchyard, near Broadstairs. The inscription on his headstone reads: 'Mr Richard Joy, the Kentish Samson, died May 18, 1742. Age 67 years. Herculean hero famed for strength/ At last lies here his breadth and length/See how the mighty man hath fallen/ To death the strong and weak all one/And the same judgement doth befall/ Goliath great and David small'.

SALTWOOD

Croft, James (1784-1869). Archdeacon. He held 27 church livings, a number of them at the same time. He was Rector of Saltwood, 1812 until death, Rector of Cliffe-at-Hoo, 1818 until death, and Archdeacon of Canterbury, 1825 until death at Saltwood Rectory. He restored Saltwood Church, 1847. Curiously he objected to seeing tombs and headstones from the Rectory windows at Saltwood and, according to Igglesden in Vol.23 of 'A Saunter Through Kent' Croft started to have the stones removed. A parishioner named Collyer objected, took the case to the law courts and won, so the headstones of the Collyers and some other families survived. Ironically, however, when Croft died a large tomb was erected over his own grave in the churchyard — in full view of the Rectory windows! Perhaps it was his way of getting revenge from beyond the grave.

SANDHURST

Nesfield, Vincent (1879-1972). Doctor. F.R.C.S. He pioneered the sterilisation of drinking water by chlorine. Dr Nesfield was an outstanding and at times unorthodox surgeon and G.P. ahead of his time. He more than anyone was responsible for the sterilisation of water, an enormous benefit to mankind. This began when as a young man he was a doctor with the Indian Army. His other 'specialities' were eyes, backs and some forms of cancer. When Esmond Knight, the actor, was blinded in action on H.M.S. *Prince of Wales* all the well-known London eye specialists said they could do nothing, but Nesfield agreed to treat him and eventually gave him back sufficient sight for Knight to continue his acting career. This remarkable achievement had a sequel many years later when an R.N.L.I. lifeboat (financed by a grateful cured cancer patient) was named *Vincent Nesfield* at Eastbourne by Esmond Knight. During 48 years at Cowbeach in Sandhurst parish he was local G.P., had consulting rooms in Harley Street and ran his own nursing home in Sandhurst. A very religious man, his medical approach was dominated by his conviction of the need to heal body *and* soul. Interred with his wife Grace (d.1972) in St Nicholas' Churchyard, Sandhurst. (See Boughton Monchelsea—Tomkin)

Pertwee, Roland (1885-1963). Author. Playwright. Father of Jon Pertwee, actor, and Michael Pertwee, dramatic writer. His plays include 'Heatwave', 'The Paragon' and 'Pink String & Sealing Wax'. Interred in St Nicholas' Churchyard, Sandhurst.

SANDWICH

Boys, William (1735-1803). Historian. Antiquarian. Topographer. Author of 'History of Sandwich'. Interred near the step before the altar rail, with his second wife, Jane, in St Clement's Church, Sandwich.

SEAL

Pratt, Sir Charles (1713-1794). 1st Earl Camden. Lord Chancellor. Chief Justice of Common Pleas. When Attorney-General he figured in the trial of the Irish-born spy Florence Hensey, who was paid 100 guineas a year to inform France of the English Fleet's movements. The suspicions of a letter-deliverer were aroused by Hensey's numerous letters from France. Some letters were opened, and he was arrested, tried as a traitor and sentenced to death. The execution was never carried out, because after it had been postponed twice and Hensey was allowed bail when the case went to appeal he disappeared. Interred in St Peter & St Paul's Church, Seal.

Pratt, Sir John (1656-1724/5?). Judge. Lawyer. Lord Chief Justice of the Court of the King's Bench. A sound and brilliant career was besmirched by his brutal treatment of the Jacobite Christopher Layer, whom he ordered to kept in heavy irons in the Tower pending trial although Layer was suffering from strangury (painful urination). Charles, his third son (see above) by his second wife, eclipsed his fame as a lawyer and was created 1st Earl Camden. Interred in St Peter & St Paul's Church, Seal.

SELLINDGE

Heyman, Sir Peter (1580-1641). Politician. Soldier. He served in Elizabeth's army and was knighted by James I for service in Ireland. M.P. for Hythe in Charles I's reign, but he opposed this king's policies and demands for money. For this and for refusing to pay a fine he was sent on Government work in Germany at his own expense. When the Speaker, Sir John Finch, his own cousin (see Canterbury—Finch) refused to allow the reading of a resolution on taxation and tried to leave the Chair and suspend the sitting of Parliament in March 1629, Heyman said he was sorry the Speaker was a Kentish man 'and that you are of that name which hath borne some good reputation in our own country'. He even suggested the Speaker should be called to the Bar of the House and a new Speaker chosen. For this Heyman, on the king's orders, was committed to the Tower but eventually released. He was elected to the Long Parliament representing Dover in 1640. In 1646 Parliament granted £5,000 to his heirs for his loss and suffering under the king and for services he did the Commonwealth. Interred in St Mary the Virgin's Church, Sellindge, but there is no known monument or grave site. The impressive tomb with kneeling figure between the Sanctuary and Lady Chapel is that of Ralph Heyman (d.1601).

SEVENOAKS

Braithwaite, John (d.1717). Head Coachman to the 1st Duke of Dorset, Knole, killed when he fell from his coach at Riverhead. A stone outside St Nicholas Church, Sevenoaks, beneath a window at the east end of the Chantry Chapel, tells of the tragic death, but it is unknown whether Braithwaite was interred in the vicinity.

Dickens, Mary ('Mamie') (1838-1896). Daughter of Charles Dickens. Author of 'My Father as I recall him', which was published several months after her death. Interred in St Nicholas' Churchyard, Sevenoaks.

Lambarde, William (1536-1601). Author of the first ever county history 'A Perambulation of Kent', published 1576. Antiquarian, but in his lifetime better known for his books on the law and for being Keeper of the Rolls (National Records) to Elizabeth I. He married three times: Jane Multon, m.1570, of Ightham (see Ightham—Lambarde); Sylvestra Dallison, m.1583, and Margaret Reder, m.1592. Lambarde had three sons and one daughter by his second wife. Interred originally in Greenwich Church, but during its rebuilding his monument was removed to St Nicholas' Church, Sevenoaks, where his descendants lived. It is probable that his body was removed at the same time and re-interred in the Lambarde vault in Sevenoaks Church.

SHADOXHURST

Lee, James (Jimmy) (1793-1865). A self-educated Farm Labourer who became a prominent Wesleyan Preacher in East Kent in 1819 until his death. Edward Pearson, another self-educated Farm Labourer and admirer of Lee, wrote Lee's biography in 1869, in doggerel comprising 1,200 verses. It is said that Lee entered Kingsnorth Church and was so impressed by the sermon that he decided to devote the rest of his life to the cause of Christ. Instead of being opposed by the local Anglican incumbent as was often the case, Lee was on friendly terms with the Vicar of Shadoxhurst and they arranged that their services should not clash, the chapel being shut when the church service was held and vice-versa. Lee's views on temperance were known throughout a wide area and men coming out of public houses were known to jump over hedges and devise other means of avoiding meeting him face to face. Interred in St Peter & St Paul's Churchyard, Shadoxhurst, on the north side of the church, the headstone being paid for by public subscription.

Molloy, Sir Charles (1684-1760). Captain of the Royal Yachts *William & Mary* and *May*, and appointed Captain of the *Royal Caroline* by George II. Director of Greenwich Hospital, Elder Brother of Trinity House and also a J.P. for Kent. There is a fine monument to him in white marble with his life story on the north wall of the chancel of St Peter & Paul's Church, Shadoxhurst. Molloy's tomb with iron railings is in the churchyard near the north-east corner of the chancel.

Rolfe Children. Oldham (d.1849, aged 9 months), William (d.1858, aged 5 years), Elizabeth (d.1858, aged 2 years 8 months), Lydia (d.1861, aged 1 year 11 months). The four children listed are interred beneath four almost illegible small stone caskets in the extreme south-west corner of the churchyard, close to the old stone wall of the school. Their father, Charles (1802-77) was Vicar of Shadoxhurst and is buried with his wife Lydia (1819-1905) close to the porch of St Peter & St Paul's Church, Shadoxhurst. Their elder brother Charles (1847-1922) did reach manhood, and took over the living from his father. He is interred with his wife Ellen (1846-1927) and infant daughter Alice (d.1878, aged 6 months) also near the church porch. (See Badlesmere— Walker children; Cooling—Comport children)

SHIPBOURNE

Vane, Sir Henry, the Elder (1589-1655). He held various government offices including that of Secretary of State, but was dismissed from his appointments by Charles I, 1641. He therefore joined the Parliamentary faction and remained with Parliament after Charles' execution, 1649. Interred in the crypt of St Giles' Church, Shipbourne. (See entry for his son and how retribution was meted out to him for his father's 'sins'.)

Lord Dunsany's grave at Shoreham. (Photograph by courtesy of Kenneth Miller, Beckenham)

The grave of Shoreham artist Harold Copping, in St Peter & St Paul's Churchyard, Shoreham. (Photograph by courtesy of Kenneth Miller, Beckenham)

Vane, Sir Henry, the Younger (1613-1662). Statesman. Writer. He emigrated to Massachusetts in 1635 and became Governor in 1636. He supported Parliament but later, having quarrelled with Oliver Cromwell, was imprisoned in 1656, but released on Cromwell's death, two years later. On the Restoration of Charles II, 1660, he was arrested, accused of high treason and beheaded in June 1662 on Tower Hill, the scene being witnessed by Samuel Pepys. Interred in the crypt of St Giles' Church, Shipbourne.

SHOREHAM

Copping, Harold (1864-1932). Painter, Illustrator. One of the group known as 'the Shoreham artists'. His pictures of Bible scenes and events were used in churches and Sunday Schools here and in mission stations in British colonies overseas. His memorial in the church refers to this: 'his pictures inspired the religious imagination of people of many races'. Interred in St Peter & St Paul's Churchyard, Shoreham.

Dunsany, Lord Edward John Moreton Drax Plunkett (1878-1957). 18th Baron Dunsany. Poet. Playwright. Short Story Writer. Author. Interred in St Peter & St Paul's Churchyard, Shoreham.

SHORNCLIFFE

Brennan, Joseph Charles (1818-1872). Victoria Cross Winner. Bombardier (later Sgt.) Royal Regt. of Artillery. He won his V.C. on 3rd April 1858, during the Indian Mutiny. He died at Elham but was interred in the Military Cemetery, Shorncliffe, though there is no headstone marking the grave.

Doogan, John (1853-1940). Victoria Cross Winner. Private, 1st Dragoon Guards. He won his V.C. in South Africa on 28th January 1881. He died at Folkestone but was interred in the Military Cemetery, Shorncliffe. (See Beckenham—Evans; Canterbury—Byrne; and other V.C. winners)

McHale, Patrick (1826-1866). Victoria Cross Winner. Private, 1st Bn., 5th Regt. (later Northumberland Fusiliers). He won his V.C. during the Indian Mutiny on 2nd October and 22nd December 1857. Interred in Plot H in the Military Cemetery, Shorncliffe.

SITTINGBOURNE

Lushington, Thomas (1590-1661). Theologian. Chaplain to the Bishop of Oxford, then to Charles I who gave him preferments to several Suffolk and Norfolk Churches, but he was deprived of these in the Civil War, so lived quietly 'publishing divers books (on theology) to gain money for his maintenance'. At the Restoration he declined several preferments due to age and apparently died at the home of a kinsman near Sittingbourne. Interred in the south chancel, St Michael's Church, Sittingbourne, on 26th December 1661. (See Norton—Lushington)

Phillipe, Jean, the Comte de Cacqueray (d.1802). French Nobleman. Refugee. For some reason unknown he was expelled from France but was eventually given permission to return. On his journey home, presumably to Dover, he died at Sittingbourne. Interred in St Michael's Churchyard, Sittingbourne.

SMARDEN

Wilmot, John (d.early 19th century?). In Vol.VI of his 'A Saunter Through Kent' published 1904, in the chapter concerning Smarden, Igglesden states: 'About a hundred years ago a sailor named John Wilmot ascended the tower (the square red-brick tower of Romden "Castle" between Smarden and Bethersden) and threw himself to the ground. He died soon after from his injuries and was buried close to the east end of Smarden Church where his tombstone, held against the wall by two iron clasps, can still be seen. It used to be said that the grass never grew on the spot where the body alighted and that the marks of the poor fellow's feet remained. This was near the tower on the south-west side. But it so happened that everyone who went to the spot habitually placed their feet on the bare spot and this, not any miraculous cause, prevented the grass from growing. The present occupier, Mr Buss, removed the flattened turf and replaced it with new turf and this grew as strong as the grass around it, so no truth in the old superstition.' By Igglesden's calculation this took place around 1804, but the dates on the headstone to which he refers do not agree. The Rev. Francis Haslewood in his 'Memorials of Smarden', 1886, which recorded all the gravestone inscriptions then in the church and churchyard, states: 'On the East wall of the chancel (in the churchyard): John Wilmot, died February 7th, 1854, aged 84. Margaret, his wife, died October 3rd, 1813, aged 44 years. John, their Son, died April 15th, 1817, aged 25 years. Left surviving William, Mary, Thomas, Robert, Jane and Margaret.' This is the only example of a grave to John Wilmot listed by Haslewood in Smarden Churchyard, nor does he mention in his pages concerning the history of Romden 'Castle' the suicide of John Wilmot there. In his transcriptions of the parish registers also published in his book he does not list among the appropriate dates the interments of the two John Wilmots or Margaret Wilmot, but this does not mean they were not interred at Smarden or recorded in the parish register. It is possible he did not know of Wilmot's suicide if it occurred some eighty or so years earlier, or if he did he may have thought it undesirable to record such an event in his scholarly book. If the tragedy did take place as Igglesden relates it seems probable it *was* the decease of John Wilmot the son in 1817. But where did Igglesden get his 'information' to refer to in his usually well-researched books? Did some local inhabitant spin the questioning young Igglesden a yarn, or did an elderly Smarden resident, who may have been told the 'information' when young by a parent or relative living at the time of the young sailor Wilmot's suicide relate to Igglesden an event that had been hushed up for many a year? The answer is now impossible to discover. The only 'evidence' is the now almost illegible headstone of the two John Wilmots. (See Harbledown; High Halden; Ickham)

In Smarden Churchyard there are two separate 'oven graves' or vaults. One is a large brick vault built above ground with iron gratings and now covered with ivy. It contains four lead coffins, two of which are visible through the gratings, one having the top badly dented. On a stone set into the east wall an inscription that is almost illegible states: 'In this vault are deposited the remains of Hannah Woolley who departed this life 21st of December, 1788, aged 32 years. Likewise of John and Frances Woolley, Father and Mother of the above. Frances Woolley died the 11th of May, 1803, aged 85. John Woolley died the 20th of February, 1818, aged 87 years. They left issue one son John Charles. Also of John Charles Woolley whose mortal life was closed the 3rd of October, 1818, aged 57 years.' The other, smaller 'oven vault', has the visible arched brickwork low down but it is not possible to see within it. A stone bears an illegible inscription but it may be the grave of Thomas Farley, yeoman, died 1822, aged 73 and Mary Farley, his wife, died 1832, aged 77. This 'oven vault' has a large tree growing out of it. There are also 'oven graves' at Biddenden, Tenterden, Bethersden, Folkestone (see also).

SMEETH

Scott or Scot, Reginald or Reynold (as he signed his name) (1538-1599). In 1574 he published 'A Perfect Platform of a Hoppe Garden and Necessary Instructions for the Making and Maintenance thereof with Notes and Rules for Reformation of all Abuses', the first practical treatise on hop culture in England that is said to have done much to stimulate hop growing in Kent. He was born at the now-vanished Scots Hall, Smeeth, a member of the twelve generations of a distinguished family that lived there. Author, after much research and personal investigation at courts of law trying witches and in rural areas among superstitious villagers, of 'The Discoverie of Witchcraft wherein the Lewde dealing of Witches and Witchmongers is notablie detected, in 16 books, wherewith is added a Treatise upon the Nature and Substance of Spirits and Devils', 1584. Scott championed the so-called 'witches' and he endeavoured to demonstrate that there were no such things as magic and witchcraft. He laid the blame for the continuing belief in them at the door of the Roman Catholic Church which, he said, played on the gullibility of ignorant people. He also tried by his book to protect the poor, aged and simple-minded from persecution. The book had a good reception and for a time resulted in a more humane outlook until James, King of Scots, denounced it in 'Daemonology'. The last words of his Will, drawn up less than a month before he died, stated 'Great is the trouble my poor wife hath had with me and small is the comfort she hath received at my hands, whom if I had not matched withal I had not died worth one groat'. Interred in St Mary's Church, Smeeth.

SNODLAND

Waghorn, Thomas Fletcher (1800-1850). Lieut. R.N. Pioneer of the overland route to India. Having joined the Navy in 1812 he could find no employment there when he finished his training five years later because of the run-down of the Navy after the Napoleonic Wars. He therefore became Third Mate on a merchant ship trading to Calcutta. In 1819 he was appointed to the Bengal Marine Pilot Service and served in the Company's cutter in the First Burmese War, 1824. This Indian experience suggested the idea of a steamship service with India, but coal was too costly at Suez for a service via the Red Sea. He found a way of transporting it much more cheaply from Cairo to Suez so it could be sold at £4 a ton instead of £20. He set up stations along the route and paid Arabs to carry coal on their camels. A test voyage camel transport scheme, 1829, was successful in cutting time and cost. In 1841 he gave up directing the operation at Cairo and returned to London where he had established a shipping and forwarding business in 1837. He was author of several pamphlets: 'Particulars of an Overland Journey from London to Bombay by Way of the Continent, Egypt and the Red Sea', 1831, and 'Overland Mails to India and China', 1843. A statue to him stands near

Chatham railway station, the figure pointing as if to his overland route, but unfortunately in the wrong direction. He died destitute, since his expenditure on government service had not been refunded. He was interred outside the vestry door, All Saints' Church, Snodland.

SOUTHBOROUGH

Codner, Elizabeth (1824-1919). Author of the hymns 'Lord I hear of showers of blessings' and 'Jesus stood on the shore'. Interred with her mother Betsey Harris (d.1885) and her son Daniel John Drew Codner (d.1913) in St Peter's Churchyard, Southborough Common.

Mitchell, Albert (d.1897). He took part in the Charge of the Light Brigade. A Trooper, later Sgt., 13th Hussars. On leaving the army he was a Riding Instructor Constable, Kent County Constabulary. Interred in St Peter's Churchyard, Southborough Common. His memorial has been beautifully restored by the Tunbridge Wells Civic Society. (See Brenchley—Ruxton; Lympne—Damer-Dawson)

O'Rourke, Frances Eliza (d.1901). Murder Victim, aged 7½ years. While she was returning from an errand she was murdered by twenty-year-old Harold Apted, carman, of Tonbridge, on 31st December 1901. Her almost naked body was found in Vauxhall Pond. She had been sexually assaulted, then her left jugular vein severed with a sheath knife that was found still entangled in her hair where she had been dumped. Apted was arrested, tried, found guilty, sentenced to death and hanged in Maidstone Prison on 18th March 1902. On 6th January 1902 Frances was interred in St Peter's Churchyard, on the Common, Southborough. The top of her gravestone has been vandalised but the lower part still relates her name and other details. (See Hoath—Steed; Hoo St Werburgh—White; Ightham—Luard; Newington-next-Sittingbourne—Bouser; Throwley—Sondes)

SOUTHFLEET

Sedley, Sir John (d.1638). Sheriff of Kent to James I. In his Will in 1637 he left £500 to found a Free School in Southfleet, the old brick front of which still survives and is in use as a primary school. His third son was Sir Charles Sedley (1639-1701), also a benefactor of the School, being playwright, poet, song writer, critic and profligate wit at the Restoration Court and a favourite of Charles II. Sir John was interred in the Sedley south chancel, St Nicholas's Church, Southfleet.

STANSTED

Hickson, William Edward (1803-1870). Educational Writer. Editor. Publisher. Pioneer in education and social reform. Composer and Pioneer in popular music culture. In 1840 he purchased the 'Westminster Review' which he edited until 1852. In this public surveys of schools systems and surveys and reports of living conditions ·were published. He published 'The Singing Master', 1836, with his 'God Bless Our Native Land', 'Join Now in Praise and Sing' and 'Now to Heav'n Our Cry (Prayers) Ascending'. In 1836 he had written 'God Bless Our Native Land' as a new National Anthem. The opening stanza of this is: 'God Bless our native land! May Heaven's protecting hand Still guard our shore! May peace her power extend Foe be transformed to friend And Britain's rights depend On war no more'. He was related by marriage to Sydney Waterlow (see below). Interred in St Mary the Virgin's Churchyard, Stansted, tomb to the south of the church about twenty-five feet from it and opposite the more westerly of the two nave windows.

Waterlow, Sir Sydney Hedley (1822-1906). 1st Baron Waterlow. Philanthropist. Founder with his brothers in 1844 of a printing business that in 1876 became Waterlow & Sons Ltd. He worked to improve the living and sanitary conditions of the London poor. In 1863 he originated the Improved Industrial Dwellings Co. Ltd of which he was chairman until he died, when it owned 6,000 tenements housing 30,000 persons. Lord Mayor of London, 1872. Liberal M.P. for Maidstone, 1874-1880, and Gravesend 1880-1885. Vice-Chairman of the London, Chatham & Dover Railway, 1880. Related by marriage to W.E. Hickson (see above) through marrying Anna Maria Hickson, 1845. Interred in St Mary the Virgin Churchyard, Stansted, near the southern boundary of the churchyard approximately in line with the vestry. There is an impressive monument on the grave, the two ends being connectd by a slab of black marble. On one side of the latter are the words: 'Rejoice with them that do rejoice' and a picture in the centre of a father playing with two small children; on the other side are the words 'and weep with them that weep' and another central picture. Several years ago the monument was vandalised, when two lead angels and four roses were stolen.

STOCKBURY

Gover, Thomas (1594-1620). On the north side of St Mary Magdalene's Churchyard, Stockbury, near the ancient yew tree, is a headstone some 2½ feet high and 1½ feet wide, to a young man who died in 1620. This is one of the oldest gravestones outside a church in a Kent churchyard which is still legible. The inscription, in a recessed panel headed at the top with a skull and crossbones, is cut entirely in capital letters, and reads: 'Here Lieth the Body of Thomas, the Sonn of Thomas and Elizabeth Gover, who departed this life the Fifteenth of November, 1620, being aged 26 years and 3 months. This young man the people loved. He changed this life for Heaven above'. The yew tree no doubt has played a part in preserving the lettering and stone. (See Cranbrook—Courthope; Hollingbourne—Reynolds)

Far from India the Needle-like column on the grave of Mungo Park's youngest son, Archibald Park, at Stone near Dartford. (Photograph by courtesy of Kenneth Miller, Beckenham)

Ruffin, Jane (d.1660, aged 22). Childbirth Fatality. Wife of John Ruffin of Raynham. She is depicted with her sisters on the brass of her mother Dorothy Hooper (d.1648) nearby. The marble floor slab is inscribed with the rather poignant verse: 'Stay friend and read this wonder, Here lyes one Death conquered not, Whoe is and is not gone For when her leas ranne out through travaile paine Shee then surrendered and renewed againe And by her infant's birth which was her death Shee breath'd her last to give her infant breath'. Interred in the chancel of St Mary Magdalene's Church, Stockbury, close to the altar, but this is probably not the floor slab's original position as prior to the 1836 restoration of the church it is known the marble slabs and brasses now inside the communion rail were in various other positions in the floor of the chancel. (See Hartlip—Coppin)

STONE

Park, Archibald (d.1867). Lt.-Col., 29th Bengal Native Infantry. Last surviving son of Mungo Park, the African explorer. Brother of Thomas Park, Midshipman, H.M.S. *Sybille* who obtained leave and went to find out more about their father's death at Boussa but after travelling 200 miles upriver contracted fever and died, October 1827. Archibald Park is interred in St Mary's Churchyard, Stone near Dartford.

113

STURRY

Franckleyn, Katherine (d.1552). Her epitaph on a brass wall tablet in St Nicholas' Church, Sturry, is composed in an unusual style. If readers take the first letters of each line and the others underlined they discover the name of the deceased Katherine Franckleyn, who is interred in the church. This is also a very early reference to India on a Kent memorial tablet.

This rim if thou read deliberately

The body, that here lyeth buried in tombe

Know this, O thou this world, that holdeth so I lyef
As flowers that fade, thy time doth pass and wear
And though thou get the treasures of India
To the earth yet shall thou leave them again
Have in mind, now then thy baylywike alac
Ere tyme untimely tourn thee on thee back
Remember, I say, the power and the miserable
In this transitory life, as thou art able
Nought hither brought thee, nought hence mayst you carry
Ensurd, to thee, so this, is they gain.

Whose name to know thou shalt full soon

Dyed in the year of Christ 1552

SUNDRIDGE

Damer, Anne Seymour (d.1828). Sculptress. Friend of Horace Walpole and many other eminent people of her time, including Queen Caroline. There are two bust examples of her work in Sundridge Church, one of Lady Campbell, the other of the Duchess of Argyll. On her death her working tools, apron and the ashes of her favourite dog were placed in her coffin. Interred in the chancel of St Mary's Church, Sundridge.

The Mompesson Family and Causes of Death. On the left of Sundridge Churchyard as the church is approached is a large boxform grave of various members of the Mompesson family which has inscriptions that are unusual because they state the actual causes of death, rather than the common 'died after years of pain bravely borne', or similar. That of Henry Mompesson is in Latin which translates as 'Henry Mompesson second son of Sir Roger Mompesson of Durnford in the county of Dorsetshire (this was either a geographical inaccuracy or there have been considerable changes in the county boundary since then as it is now in Wiltshire—A.M.), who for a period of nearly six years suffered severely from a wasting disease of the lungs and having tried all remedies in his own country in vain, was advised to seek the milder climate of Provence where he was persuaded to remain and have

The curious shaped tomb surmounted by a vase above the vault of Bishop Beilby
Porteus at Sundridge.   (Photograph by courtesy of Kenneth Miller, Beckenham)

recourse to treatment. Whilst he was making this journey, on the 10th
September, 1723, in the port of Iccio (Nice), he was set upon by six ruffians
who attacked him with stones while he was totally unprepared and robbed him
of his money. They most foully slit his throat and left him for dead. He
lingered with this injury for 48 hours and then piously rendered up his spirit in
the 26th year of his age. Most beloved, while he lived, his remains having been
brought back from France for burial this monument was established and cared
for by his sorrowing only brother, T.M.' The left-hand panel of this side of the
tomb also records: 'Here lye also the Bodies of Alice, late wife of Thomas
Mompesson of this Parish, Esq., who died May 9th, 1747, aged 47 of a
Cancer in her Breast which she bore with Great Patience and Resignation.
And of Anne, Daughter of Edward Clavell of Dorsetshire, Esq., near-kins-
woman of the said Thomas Mompesson who dyed of the smallpox by inoculation 2nd June, 1757, aged 34. And of Thomas Mompesson, Esq., who died
May the 12th, 1767, in the 72nd year of his age.' The interesting point is
Anne's death 'of the smallpox by inoculation'. Edward Jenner did not
introduce his scientific vaccination technique of immunisation against smallpox until 1796. The inoculation that caused Anne Clavell's death was
probably the hit-or-miss system introduced by Lady Mary Wortley Montagu
(1689-1762) from Turkey earlier in the century. Benjamin Jesty (1737-1816),
a farmer in Dorset, in 1774 successfully inoculated his wife, who lived to 84,

and two sons, an Abigail Brown and various others in the locality with cowpox virus as a protection against smallpox, which is recorded on his headstone in Worth Matravers Churchyard, Dorset. (See Goudhurst—Freeman; Hothfield —Stanford; Pluckley—Nepecker)

Porteus, Beilby (1731-1809). Bishop of London. Author of various religious works. His American parents came to England in 1720, so that their children would have a better education. In 1762 he was Domestic Chaplain to the Archbishop of Canterbury, Dr Secker. In 1769 he was appointed Chaplain to the King and in 1787 became Bishop of London. He encouraged the establishment of Sunday Schools in every parish. He worked to secure the observance of religious holidays and was involved in the welfare of negro slaves in the West Indies. In 1807 at his own expense he built a chapel of ease, wth a house for the Minister, in Sundridge, where he himself stayed in summer. Interred in a vault surmounted by an imposing tomb with a vase, surrounded by high railings enclosing it like a miniature garden, the stone having been recently restored, south-east of the church in St Mary's Churchyard, Sundridge. By his own wish, only the dates of his own birth and death and those of his wife Margaret are stated, but fuller details are on the stone entrance to the vault.

SUTTON-AT-HONE

Smith (Smythe), Sir Thomas (1558-1625). Merchant. First Governor of the East India Company on its foundation in 1600, for 4 months. Re-elected each year from 1603 until 1621, apart from 1606-7. Endowed the Free School at Tonbridge originally founded by his grandfather, Sir Andrew Judd. In 1604 he was Special Ambassador to the Tsar of Russia. He provisioned and supported voyages to try and discover the North-West Passage, his name being given by William Baffin to Smith's Sound. From 1609 to 1620 he was Commissioner for the Navy and Treasurer of the Virginia Company, but was suspected of embezzling from the Virginia Company, a charge of which he was later found to be innocent. Interred beneath an elaborate monument in St John the Baptist's Church, Sutton-at-Hone.

SUTTON VALENCE

Willes, John (1777-1852). Cricketer. He taught the famous Alfred Mynn (see Thurnham) to bowl. It was his sister's skill in throwing the ball to him when practising in a barn at Tonford near Canterbury that suggested to him the idea of re-introducing round-arm bowling (another bowler had tried for a short time years before but failed). Reputedly his sister Christina at first bowled to him underarm as was usual but she found the ball became caught in her wide flowing skirt and so she whirled the ball over her head, and to her and her brother's surprise sent down a ball at great speed. Impressed, he tried round-arm bowling in the match at Lords between Kent and the MCC in 1822. He was no-balled, so threw down the ball, mounted his horse and rode home saying he would never play again, but he did, when opposition to this bowling was overcome. He kept a pack of hounds, went fox-hunting and shooting, was considered the best shot and amateur boxer in the county of his time. Interred in St Mary's Churchyard, Sutton Valence, to the left side of the church path, as the church door is approached from the east end.

SWANSCOMBE

Weldon, Anthony (1548-1613). Brother of Sir Ralph Weldon (see below). A member of the Weldon family who passed on his royal appointment to his nephew, also Anthony, son of Ralph. The epitaph on the memorial tablet on the wall of the Lady Chapel in St Peter & St Paul's Church, Swanscombe, reads: 'Here lieth the body of Anthony Weldon, younger son to Anthony Weldon, who died Clerk of the Greencloth to Queen Elizabeth and brother to Ralph Weldon who died in the same office to King James, himself being Clerk of the Kitchen to both Elizabeth and James who voluntarily and freely resigned the same place to his nephew, Anthony Weldon, now Clerk to the Kitchen in the second year of his reign. As in his life he showed himself kind and loving to his said nephew so at his death he made him sole executor, in grateful memory whereof he hath erected this small monument. He died 12th April in the year, 1613, in the reign of King James I, at the age of 65.'

Weldon, Sir Ralph (1545-1609). The epitaph on his tomb relates the remarkable number of royal offices the Weldon family held in several reigns in succession: 'To the grateful memory of Sir Ralph Weldon, Knight, whose body lies here entombed. His wife, the late Eliza Weldon, out of her dear affection and respect erects this monument to show how: He was Chief Clerk of the Kitchen to Queen Elizabeth afterward Clerk Comptroller to King James and died Clerk of the Greencloth on the 12th November in the year 1609 and of his age of 64, having by the said Eliza, daughter to Leven Buffkin, Esq., 4 sons: Anthony, Clerk of the Kitchen to James I; Henry; Leven; and Ralph. 6 daughters: Katherine, Ann, Elizabeth, Mary, Judith and Barbara. His grand-father, Edward Weldon, served King Henry 7 and was Master of the Household to King Henry 8, whom likewise his uncle, Thomas Weldon, served and was Cofferer to King Edward 6 and Queen Elizabeth. Anthony Weldon, his father, likewise served Queen Elizabeth and died Clerk of the Greencloth' (duties of this office unknown). Sir Ralph's son, Anthony, who had inherited from his uncle, Anthony, later ended his association with monarchy and became anti-royalist. This was through being sacked as Clerk of the Kitchen by James I for 'having libelled the nation to which the King belonged'. This Anthony Weldon actively supported Cromwell, serving as the infamous Leader of the County Committee that controlled Kent from 1642 to 1648, but through his violent, dictatorial methods he was overthrown in the Kentish Rebellion of 1648. He wrote 'A Catt May Look At A King or a Brief Chronicle and Characters of the Kings of England from William the

Conqueror to the reign of Charles I' and 'The Secret History of the First Two Stuart Kings'. Sir Ralph Weldon's tomb stands against the south wall inside St Peter & St Paul's Church, Swanscombe.

Wilson, Sir William James Erasmus (1809-1884). Surgeon. Philanthropist. He specialised in skin diseases after 1840 and advocated to Victorians regular bathing, specially with Turkish baths, to keep skin healthy. At his own expense of £30,000 he built a new wing and chapel at the Sea Bathing Infirmary, Margate, to treat skin diseases. He invested in gas and railway companies which made him wealthy. He also became interested in Egyptian antiquities and in 1877-78 paid the expense, about £10,000, of transporting 'Cleopatra's Needle' to London's Thames Embankment in honour of his father, William Wilson, parish surgeon at Dartford and Greenhithe, who had been present during Nelson's Egyptian Campaign. He also paid for the restoration of Swanscombe Parish Church, 1873. He died at Westgate-on-Sea but is interred in the railed-off ornate marble tomb in the north aisle of St Peter & St Paul's Church, Swanscombe.

TENTERDEN

Ward, Rev. Philip (d.1859). Husband of Lord Nelson's daughter, Horatia. While Vicar of Tenterden, 1830-1859, he was involved in a quarrel over tithes between himself and his parishioners that led to a lawsuit settled by a compromise in 1842. Interred in the family vault in St Mildred's Churchyard, Tenterden, between the chancel and the Woolpack Inn. Horatia, after his death, moved to Pinner where she died and was interred, 1881, aged 80.

TESTON

Nestor (1750-1786). A Negro Slave who became the Servant of Rev. James Ramsey, one of the Abolition of Slavery Movement founders. He was brought back to Teston from the West Indies by Ramsey when 14, served Ramsey for 22 years as Servant and friend, being accepted also by all Ramsey's friends and acquaintances. There is a memorial tablet to him, erected in 1893, on the wall of the churchyard of St Peter & St Paul's Church, Teston, where he was interred on 26th December 1786.

Ramsey, Rev. Dr James (1733-1789). Rector of Teston 1781-1789. Surgeon. Joined the Royal Navy and served on the *Arundel* in the West Indies, where the conditions of the slaves arriving by ship converted him to assisting in ending the slave trade. He took Holy Orders and returned to St Kitts, West Indies, 1762. Here he assisted and taught the negroes, rousing the anger of the white settlers, so that he had to return to England where he accepted the living of Teston. In 1784 he published his 'Essay on the Treatment and Conversion of African Slaves in British Sugar Colonies' and wrote numerous other pamphlets. He gained the interest of William Wilberforce and advised Pitt and others involved in the abolition movement, much of the planning of the

Abolition Bill being done at Teston. He died two months after the Abolition Bill was introduced in Parliament by Wilberforce. Interred in St Peter & St Paul's Church, Teston.

TEYNHAM

Honeyball, Col. James Frederick (d.1923). The last private owner of New-gardens, the house and estate that was probably the residence of Richard Harris, Henry VIII's 'fruiterer' who established cherry orchards in the Teynham area (see Fordwich—Harris). Col. Honeyball was Commanding Officer of a Battalion of the East Kent Volunteers and after buying the house and estate restored both. It was visited by the Duke of York in 1922, but after the death of Mrs Honeyball and neglect by her sons, now both deceased, the vandalised house was demolished in the early 1970s to make way for a housing estate. Interred in St Mary's Churchyard, Teynham.

THROWLEY

Harris, George Robert Canning (1851-1932). 4th Lord. Cricket Player. Politician. Played for Kent 1870-1911: Captain 1875-1889. Captained England in 1880 and 1884 and in Australia 1878-79. President M.C.C. 1895. A dominant, somewhat fearsome character, concerning discipline and the game, who played his last game at Lords in 1929. Editor of 'History of Kent County Cricket'. Under-Secretary for India. Under-Secretary for War. Governor of Bombay. Interred in the Harris enclosure in the north-west corner of St Michael & All Angels Churchyard, Throwley.

Sondes, Sir George (1600-1677). Earl of Faversham. Father of the murderer Freeman Sondes and murder victim George Sondes (see below and Bearsted). Interred in a black marble chest tomb, with a very lengthy inscription, in the Sondes Chapel, St Michael & All Angels Church, Throwley.

Sondes, George (d.1655). Murder Victim. Elder son of Sir George Sondes, Earl of Faversham. Murdered by his younger brother Freeman Sondes (see Bearsted—Sondes). The burial register states: '1655. 11th August. Sonds, George, sone and appeerant haere to Sir George Sonds of Throwley, Knight of the Bathe.' Interred in the Sondes Chapel, St Michael & All Angels Church, Throwley, although there is not an inscription to this effect. (See Hoath—Steed; Hoo St Werburgh—White; Ightham—Luard; Newington-next-Sittingbourne—Bouser; Southborough—O'Rourke)

THURNHAM

Mynn, Alfred (1807-1861). Cricketer. Known as 'The Lion of Kent'. In the Kent XI for 99 matches, 1834 to 1859. Height 6 feet 1 inch, weight varying from 18 to 20 stone. 'His delivery was noble, walking majestically up to the crease though when he first began he used to advance with a run. His bowling was very fast and ripping-round-armed and of a good length.' When he died he was accorded military honours at his funeral. Interred in St Mary the

119

Virgin's Churchyard, Thurnham. The inscription records that four hundred people united to erect the tombstone and to found in his honour the Mynn Memorial Benevolent Institution for Kent cricketers with a sum of £121.16s invested in India 5 per cent Stocks for the benefit in perpetuity of the objects of the above-named charity.

TONBRIDGE

Fielding, George Hunsley (1801-1871). Doctor who recorded the hottest weather temperature in Britain. He kept daily recordings from his weather instruments and forwarded the readings to the Royal Observatory for many years. On July 22nd 1868, he recorded a shade temperature in his garden, Grove House, of 100.5°F (38.1°C), in the sun 142°F, which gained for Tonbridge the record of being the hottest place in Britain. He authenticated his recordings as thoroughly as he possibly could with the equipment available to him but it is now thought the temperature that day was more likely 97°-98°F, the difference being due to possible inaccuracies in the recording methods. Interred by the chapel, the sunny side, in Tonbridge Cemetery.

TROTTISCLIFFE

Sutherland, Graham Vivian (1903-1980). Painter. Designer. Etcher. Engraver. Official War Artist. He designed the large tapestry 'Christ in Majesty' in Coventry Cathedral, 1962. He was noted for his surrealist land-scapes. His portraits, however, were sometimes controversial, such as those of Somerset Maugham and the 80th birthday portrait of Sir Winston Churchill. Interred in St Peter & St Paul's Churchyard, Trottiscliffe.

TUNBRIDGE WELLS

Bell, Jacob (1810-1859). Founder of the Pharmaceutical Society. In 1841 he planned a society to act as a safeguard for chemists and druggists, having inherited such a business from his father. He founded the 'Pharmaceutical Journal' and wrote much of its contents, as well as being its editor, for 18 years. For the first 15 years it was a labour of love and he used his own money to finance it. He helped in drawing up an Act of Parliament to make the practice of pharmacy lawful only for qualified persons. It was not proceeded with so he became an M.P. in 1850, and in 1851 he put his own Bill before Parliament which was eventually passed. He was a friend of Sir Edwin Land-seer and Sidney Cooper and collected their paintings. On the day of his funeral virtually all the pharmacists in Britain were closed as a mark of respect. Interred near Dr Golding Bird in Trinity Cemetery, Woodbury Park Road, Tunbridge Wells.

Bird, Golding (1814-1854). Physician. Researcher into scientific medicine. He lectured on medical botany, urinary pathology and also the therapeutical uses of electricity. In 1839 he suggested a method of printing figures of natural objects by sunlight on paper impregnated with the salt ferridicyanide of potassium that anticipated later photographic processes (see Bishopsbourne—Reade). Author of 'Bird's Elements of Natural Philosophy', formerly a popular textbook for medical students. Interred near Jacob Bell in Trinity Cemetery, Woodbury Park Road, Tunbridge Wells.

Middlemore, Col. George (d.1850). He served in the 48th Foot at the Battle of Talavera. When Colonel Donnellan was mortally wounded he ordered Middlemore to lead the famous advance and charge to rescue the Guards when the Regiment won its badge of the Star of Brunswick or 'Coldstream Star'. He was Governor of St Helena at the time of the removal of Napoleon's remains in 1840. At the head of his tomb is a stone tablet telling of the Talavera event, placed there in 1907 by the 1st Northampton Regt., descendants of the 48th Foot, when the grave was restored. Interred in Trinity Cemetery, Woodbury Park Road, Tunbridge Wells.

Smirke, Sydney (1798-1877). Architect. Artist. Surveyor. In 1847 he took over from his brother Sir Robert Smirke work on the British Museum, which he finished in 1855. In 1854 he commenced the Reading Room, opened in 1857. He rebuilt the Carlton Club, London, which incorporated the first use of polished granite columns in England. He exhibited at the Royal Academy and designed and constructed the exhibition galleries at Burlington House. Interred in Trinity Cemetery, Woodbury Park Road, Tunbridge Wells.

TUNSTALL

Twopeny, William (1799-1873). Artist. Lawyer in the family business at Rochester. He specialised in antiquarian subjects and ancient churches but also drew domestic buildings of all types, copying wood and metal work and stained glass, often in fine detail. Many of the subjects he recorded have since disappeared or been much altered. The British Museum possesses a number of his drawings. The Twopeny family formerly owned the estate of Woodstock Park, Tunstall. Interred, with other members of his family, in St John the Baptist's Churchyard, Tunstall.

UPCHURCH

Bones Collection. In 1896 a collection of human bones was found in a small crypt underneath the 14th century north chancel of St Mary the Virgin's Church, Upchurch. This indicates the crypt was used as a charnel house for the storing of human bones, perhaps exhumed from the churchyard. (When space became scarce it was the custom to exhume after a period of years to allow new burials to take place. See Hythe.) The bones in the Upchurch charnel house were reburied, but at the present time the site is unknown.

WATERINGBURY

Clampard, Thomas (d.1748). Believed to have been the last holder in Kent of the Office of Deputy to the Dumb Borsholder. The latter is made of wood, about three feet long, with an iron ring at the top, four more on the sides and an iron spike four inches long at one end. It was held by the rings and used as a ram to break down doors of houses believed to contain stolen or smuggled goods. No warrant from a Justice of the Peace was needed. The Keeper of the Dumb Borsholder was a Petty Constable who had jurisdiction over a number of houses, each householder paying the Deputy to the Dumb Borsholder a penny annually, and each householder taking it in turn to act as Deputy. The two last places where this office survived were Great Chart, near Ashford, and Chart, Wateringbury. Interred in St John's Churchyard, Wateringbury. His epitaph, as he was the village blacksmith, has the familiar 'My sledge and anvil I've declined, etc.'. The Dumb Borsholder is preserved in Wateringbury Church.

Style, Sir Oliver (d.?). Diplomat. Member of the Style family of Langley, Beckenham, where there are wall memorials and interments in St George's Church. This Sir Oliver was reputed to be sitting in a room with some merchants at Smyrna when an earthquake occurred and, perceiving the house moving, he threw himself under a strong table which saved his life as the building collapsed and killed the others in the room with him. He is interred in a stone coffin in a Portland stone tomb, on the right hand side of the south porch, in St John's Churchyard, Wateringbury. On the north and south sides of it are marble tablets with long Latin inscriptions that tell the story. Other forebears of Sir Oliver are interred in Wateringbury Church.

WESTBERE

Gilbert, Thomas and Edmond (1639-1640). Twins. Below the inscription there is depicted the likeness of two boys, standing holding hands, the one on the left by his right hand holding the left hand of the other, their other arms not being shown. Nor are their heads. Although the lettering and the lower part of the boys from the shoulders down is quite deeply incised the black marble floor slab does not appear ever to have been carved where their heads should be, nor does it appear to have been worn down in that area. This raises the possibility that the heads were never incised because the twins were in fact Siamese twins joined at the head or upper shoulder. Interred on the north side of the chancel of All Saints' Church, Westbere. (See Jenkins Sisters below)

Jenkins Sisters. Across the chancel from the Gilbert Twins (see above) on the south side, is a limestone floor slab to the memory of three sisters interred beneath, placed there by a fourth sister. It reads 'Inscribed by Ann Nairn in memory of her three sisters whose mortal remains are interred beneath with their respective names as follows: Hester Jenkins, died 1808; (?) died April, 1811; Margaret, died October, 1811'. It is not possible to read some details as they are hidden by the pulpit steps. In the centre of the chancel between her sisters and the Gilbert Twins is a floor slab inscribed by the same Ann Nairn to her parents who lie beneath. Interred in the chancel of All Saints' Church, Westbere. (See Wye—Johnson Sisters)

WESTERHAM

Earning, John (1669-1688). Accident Victim. According to the inscription 'son of Anthony Earning, Marchant, who was unfortunately slaine in ye Strand over against ye New Exchange on the 18th June, 1688, in ye 19th year of his age to ye great greife of his friends'. The occasion of this accident is believed to have been during the rejoicing of the population in London after the judges' acquittal and release of the Seven Bishops who had protested against James II's policies. Interred beneath a floor slab in St Mary's Church, Westerham.

WEST WICKHAM

Morice, Burton (1766-1825). Steward and one of the Judges of the Palace Court, Westminster. Interred beneath a floor slab between the chancel and the nave in St John's Church, West Wickham.

WHITSTABLE

Smith, Alphons (d.1931). Known also as 'Trader Horn'. Author. Big-Game Hunter. Trader in ivory. After retirement to Whitstable he wrote books on his experiences under the pen-name 'Trader Horn'. He was a local character who sported a 'nanny-goat' beard and wore a large brimmed wideawake hat. Interred in Whitstable Cemetery. The gravestone bears as inscription lines from R.L. Stevenson's 'Requiem': 'Home is the sailor, home from the sea and the hunter home from the hill'.

WOODCHURCH

Waterhouse, Sir Edward (1535-1591). Chancellor of the Exchequer in Ireland to Elizabeth I. He served Sir Henry Sidney who was Lord Deputy of Ireland in 1565, and held various Irish posts. He had several rewards heaped on him that aroused Elizabeth's jealousy, especially that of Water Bailiff and Keeper of the Shannon and Custodian of the Boats at Athlone. He was ordered back to England and surrendered his post as Water Bailiff to placate Elizabeth (see Ashford—Smythe). He returned to Ireland to various duties that included being ordered by Lord Burghley to torture the Archbishop of Armagh by toasting his bare feet in front of a fire. He returned from Ireland in 1591 to his Woodchurch estate, Henden Place, to live in retirement, but he died there in October the same year. Interred in a tomb in the south chapel of All Saints' Church, Woodchurch.

WOULDHAM

Burke, Walter (1745-1815). Purser, H.M.S. *Victory*. He was on board at the Battle of Trafalgar and in his arms Lord Nelson is reputed to have died. Since 1898 children from Wouldham Primary School have paid a traditional annual visit to lay wreaths and bunches of flowers on his grave to mark the day of the famous battle. Interred near to All Saints' Church, Wouldham.

Another local seaman who served with Nelson at Trafalgar is John George Mount who is interred in nearby Frindsbury Churchyard.

WYE

Brett, Gregory (buried 1541). **Brett, Gregory** (buried 1586), his son. Their remains in the hope of a joyful resurrection are interred in a vault in the nave of Wye Church. The memorial floor slab records that Gregory Brett the son 'churchwarden 1582, 83, 84, rebuilt the old steeple burned by lightning on July 15, 1572, to which he was a great contributor by forgiving the parish a debt of £92 12 shillings and 6 pence besides his sess of £30 for which benefit they granted the burial place to him and his heirs on payment of 6 shillings and 8 pence at every interment'. Probably the vicar's interment fee? After him another fourteen Bretts or relatives by marriage were interred in the same vault, presumably all at 6 shillings and 8 pence a time, in St Gregory & St Martin's Church, Wye.

Brett, Thomas (1667-1743). Non-Juring Divine. Curate of Great Chart and Wye; Rector of Betteshanger and Ruckinge. On the accession of George I he refused to take oaths and resigned his living but continued to officiate at his house, Spring Grove, Wye. In 1718 and 1729 he was taken before the Assizes for interfering with the duties of the parish clergyman, but on each occasion was let off with a reproof. He took part in various national controversies concerned with the non-juring question. He wrote a large number of books on ecclesiastical matters, and also 'A General History of the World', 1732. Interred in St Gregory & St Martin's Church, Wye.

Johnson, Agnes (1715-1763) and **Johnson, Mary** (1719-1767). Two sisters, who both died aged 48. Daughters and co-heiresses of John Johnson of Wye and of Mary Johnson, descended from Sir Robert Moyle of Buckwell. Their memorial on the south wall of the chancel records: 'Their days were imbittered by various evils. Their conduct proves that true Christian resignation May palliate the heaviest afflictions.' One cannot but wonder what the 'evils' and 'afflictions' were. The stone was erected 'in memory of a friendship which death alone could end' by Susannah and Penelope Woodyers. Both sisters are interred in the chancel of St Gregory & St Martin's Church, Wye. (See Westbere—Jenkins Sisters)

Thornhill, Lady Joanna (1635-1708). Lady of the Bedchamber to Queen Catherine, Consort of Charles II. Sister of John, Earl of Bath, who, with his kinsman, General Monk, afterwards Duke of Albemarle, was instrumental in the Restoration of Charles II, 1660. She was second wife of Richard Thornhill, of Olantigh, Commander of a Regiment of Horse raised at his own expense in Charles I's service. Interred in the chancel of St Gregory & St Martin's Church, Wye, where she chose to be interred as a mark of respect for her husband. She left a benefaction in her Will 'to support poor House Keepers and to teach their children to read and write' as indicated on the large marble wall tablet on the south side of the chancel.

INDEX